Working Papers

FINANCIAL ACCOUNTING
THE IMPACT ON DECISION MAKERS

Prepared by
Diane L. Tanner
University of North Florida

GARY A. PORTER
LOYOLA UNIVERSITY CHICAGO

CURTIS L. NORTON
NORTHERN ILLINOIS UNIVERSITY

The Dryden Press
Harcourt Brace & Company
Fort Worth Philadelphia San Diego New York Orlando Austin San Antonio
Toronto Montreal London Sydney Tokyo

Custom Publisher Mike Beaupré
Senior Production Manager Sue Dunaway

Working Papers Financial Accounting
The Impact on Decision Makers

Printed in the United States of America
0-03-020518-2

Contents

Name________________________________
Class Time____________________________

EXERCISE 1-4

	A =	L +	OE
Case 1:	$125,000	$ 75,000	$
Case 2:	400,000		100,000
Case 3:		320,000	95,000

EXERCISE 1-5

	A =	L +	OE
1.			

	A =	L +	OE
2.			

	A =	L +	OE
3.			

	A =	L +	OE
4.			

EXERCISE 1-6

1.	A =	L +	OE
Beginning of year			
+ Net income			
- Dividends			
Owners' equity at end of year			

Name______________________________
Class Time__________________________

EXERCISE 1–6 continued

2.	A =	L +	OE
Beginning of year			
End of year			
Reduce by half to beginning of year			
Assets, beginning of year			

3.	A =	L +	OE
Beginning of year			
Triples during the year			
Liabilities, end of year			

EXERCISE 1-7

1.	A =	L +	OE
1996:	$ 25,000	$ 12,000	13,000
1997:	79,000	67,000	12,000
1998:	184,000	137,000	47,000

Change in owners' equity during 1997:

79,000 − 67,000 = 12,000
79,000 = 67,000 + 12,000

Change in owners' equity during 1998:

184,000 − 137,000 = 47,000
184,000 = 137,000 + 47,000

2. **1997:**

3. **1998:**

Name________________________________
Class Time___________________________

PROBLEM 1-1 or 1-1A

Discussion of process, risk, information needed, receipt of winnings:

Name____________________________________

Class Time_________________________________

PROBLEM 1-2 or 1-2A

	Type of Organization	Reason
1.		
2.		
3.		
4.		
5.		

Note: Problem 1-2A has only 4 parts.

Name______________________________
Class Time__________________________

PROBLEM 1-3 or 1-3A

1. ______________________________	
STATEMENT OF CASH FLOWS	
FOR THE YEAR ENDED DECEMBER _____, 1995	
(in Millions)	
Net cash provided by operations:	
Cash flows from investing activities:	
Cash flows from financing activities:	
Increase in cash and cash equivalents	

2. Other investing activities:
Other financing activities:

Name________________________________
Class Time___________________________

PROBLEM 1-4

Information	Management	Stockholders	Banker
1.			
2.			
3.			
4.			
5.			

Name________________________________

Class Time __________________________

PROBLEM 1-4A

Information	Management	Stockholders	Franchisor
1.			
2.			
3.			
4.			
5.			

Name______________________________

Class Time__________________________

PROBLEM 1-5 or 1-5A

______________________ CORPORATION			
BALANCE SHEET			
______________ 31, 1998			
Assets		Liabilities and Owners' Equity	

Items Not Shown on the Balance Sheet	Where Each Would Appear

Name________________________________

Class Time____________________________

PROBLEM 1-6 or 1-6A

1.

BALANCE SHEET	
DECEMBER 31, 1998	
Assets	Liabilities and Owners' Equity

Computations:

2. Memorandum to the company president:

TO:

FROM:

DATE:

SUBJECT:

Name______________________________
Class Time__________________________

PROBLEM 1-7 or 1-7A

1.

______________________________		
INCOME STATEMENT		
FOR THE __________ ENDED ________________,1998		
Revenues:		
Expenses:		

2.

__________________	
STATEMENT OF RETAINED EARNINGS	
FOR THE ________________ ENDED _________________,1998	
Beginning balance, ____________, 1998	
Ending balance, _____________, 1998	

PROBLEM 1-7 or 1-7A continued

3.

BALANCE SHEET			
____________________, 1998			
Assets		Liabilities and Owners' Equity	

4.

Name____________________________
Class Time________________________

PROBLEM 1-8 or 1-8A

1.

____

INCOME STATEMENT

FOR THE MONTH ENDED ____________ 31,1998

Revenues:		
Expenses:		

2.

Computations of Retained Earnings balance at ____________ 31, 1998:

____

BALANCE SHEET

____________ 31, 1998

Assets		Liabilities and Owners' Equity	

3. Information needed about notes payable:

Name_______________________________

Class Time___________________________

PROBLEM 1-9 or 1-9A

1.

INCOME STATEMENT		
FOR THE YEAR ENDED DECEMBER 31,1998		
Revenues:		
Expenses:		

2.

STATEMENT OF RETAINED EARNINGS	
FOR THE YEAR ENDED DECEMBER 31,1998	
Beginning balance, January 1, 1998	
Ending balance, December 31, 1998	

3.

BALANCE SHEET

DECEMBER 31, 1998

Assets		Liabilities and Owners' Equity	

4. Memorandum to the Company President:

TO: Company president
FROM:
DATE:
SUBJECT:

Name________________________________

Class Time____________________________

PROBLEM 1-10 or 1-10A

1.

2.

Name________________________________
Class Time____________________________

PROBLEM 1-11

Entity in Which it Occurs: B = Business NB = Nonbusiness	Accounting Knowledge Needed: F = Financial M = Managerial T = Tax NP = Not for profit
1.	
2.	
3.	
4.	
5.	
6.	
7.	
8.	
9.	
10.	

Name_______________________________
Class Time _____________________________

PROBLEM 1-11A

Position Category Is:
1.
2.
3.
4.
5.
6.
7.
8.
9.
10.
11.
12.

Name________________________________

Class Time____________________________

PROBLEM 1-12 or 1-12A

Assumptions Violated:	How Each Event Should Be Handled:

____
INCOME STATEMENT
FOR THE MONTH ENDED JULY 31,1998

Computations of owners' contributions:

PROBLEM 1-12 or 1-12A continued

BALANCE SHEET	
JULY 31, 1998	
Assets	Liabilities and Owners' Equity

Computations:

Name______________________________________

Class Time___________________________________

EXERCISE 2-1

1.	5.
2.	6.
3.	7.
4.	8.

EXERCISE 2-2

1.	4.	7.
2	5.	8.
3.	6.	9.

EXERCISE 2-3

Total Assets	=
Equity	=
Debt/Equity	=

Is the information provided by these two ratios different? Explain.

Name________________________________

Class Time____________________________

EXERCISE 2-4

	Selling (S) or General and Administrative (G & A)
Advertising expense	
Depreciation expense – store furniture and fixtures	
Office rent expense	
Office salaries expense	
Store rent expense	
Store salaries expense	
Insurance expense	
Supplies expense	
Utilities expense	

EXERCISE 2-5

	Sara's Coffee Shop	Amy's Deli	Jane's Bagels
Net sales	$35,000	$	$78,000
Cost of goods sold		45,000	
Gross profit	7,000	18,000	
Selling expenses	3,000		9,000
General and administrative expenses	1,500	2,800	
Total operating expenses		8,800	13,600
Net income	$ 2,500	$ 9,200	$25,400

EXERCISE 2-6

	Calculations	Ratio
Gross profit ratio		
Profit margin		
Earnings per share		
Return on stockholders' equity		

Other Information Needed:

Name________________________________

Class Time__________________________

EXERCISE 2-7

LANDONCORPORATION	
STATEMENT OF RETAINED EARNINGS	
FOR THE YEAR ENDED DECEMBER 31,1998	
Retained earnings, January 1, 1998	
Retained earnings, December 31, 1998	

Computation of retained earnings at December 31, 1997:		
Retained earnings, January 2, 1996		
Ending balance, December 31, 1997		

EXERCISE 2-8

	O = Operating; I = Investing; F = Financing; N = Not on the statement of cash flows
1.	
2.	
3.	
4.	
5.	
6.	
7.	
8.	

Name________________________________
Class Time___________________________

EXERCISE 2-10

	Statement		Statement
1. Accounts payable		11. Dividends	
2. Accounts receivable		12. Land held for future expansion	
3. Advertising expense		13. Loss on the sale of equipment	
4. Bad debt expense		14. Office supplies	
5. Bonds payable		15. Organizational costs	
6. Buildings		16. Patent amortization expense	
7. Cash		17. Retained earnings	
8. Common stock		18. Sales	
9. Deferred income taxes		19. Unearned revenue	
10. Depreciation expense		20. Utilities expense	

EXERCISE 2-12

Gross profit:	
Gross profit ratio:	
Profit margin:	
Earnings per share:	
Price-earnings ratio:	

Would you consider investing in Gaynor Corporation? Explain.

Name______________________________

Class Time__________________________

PROBLEM 2-1 or 2-1A

1. Accountant's perceptions of information? What action might be taken?

2. Relevance of information for hardware store or real estate company?

Name________________________________
Class Time____________________________

PROBLEM 2-2

Costs incurred	All or portion of cost on income statement and why
Display fixtures	
Advertising	
Merchandise for sale	
Costs of incorporation	
Cost of a franchise	
Office supplies	
Wages in a restaurant	
Computer software	
Computer hardware	

Name________________________________
Class Time __________________________

PROBLEM 2-2A

Costs incurred	All or portion of cost on income statement and why
Point-of-sale systems	
Ad in the yellow pages	
Computer software system	
Shipping merchandise to chain outlets	

Name____________________

Class Time____________________

PROBLEM 2-3 or 2-3A

Dear ____________________.

Name________________________________

Class Time____________________________

PROBLEM 2-5 or 2-5A

1.	December 31, 1998	December 31, 1997
a. Working capital		
b. Current ratio		

2. Liquidity evaluation:

Name______________________________

Class Time__________________________

PROBLEM 2-6 or 2-6A

1.

Current ratio	
Working capital	

2.

3.

Name________________________________

Class Time___________________________

PROBLEM 2-7 or 2-7A

Description of Transaction	Current Ratio	Effect of Transaction	Debt-to-Equity Ratio	Effect of Transaction
1. Purchase of equipment for cash				
2. Cash collections from accounts receivable				
3. Cash payment of accounts payable				
4. Cash payment				
4. Repayment of a loan				
6. Issuance of capital stock				
7. Cash dividend				

Name________________________________

Class Time____________________________

PROBLEM 2-8 or 2-8A

1.

Description of Transaction	Current Ratio	Effect of Transaction	Debt-to-Equity Ratio	Effect of Transaction
1. Purchase of equipment				
2. Cash collections from accounts receivable				
3. Cash payment of accounts payable				
4. Cash payment				
5. Repayment of a loan				
6. Issuance of capital stock for cash				
7. Cash dividend				

2. Transactions that have an indeterminable effect on the ratios:

Name______________________________

Class Time__________________________

PROBLEM 2-9 or 2-9A

1. Single-step income statement

____

INCOME STATEMENT

FOR THE YEAR ENDED DECEMBER 31, 1998

Revenues:		

2. Weaknesses in the single-step income statement:

Name______________________________

Class Time__________________________

PROBLEM 2-10 or 2-10A

1. Multiple-step income statement

____
INCOME STATEMENT
FOR THE YEAR ENDED DECEMBER 31, 1998

Revenues:		

2. Gross profit ratio =

3. What does this percentage tell you about the company's markup on its products?

Name________________________________

Class Time____________________________

PROBLEM 2-11 or 2-11A

______________________________________, INC.

STATEMENTS OF STOCKHOLDERS' EQUITY

	Number of Shares	Common Stock, Par	Paid-in Capital	Retained Earnings	Total
1/1/96					
Net income					
Dividends					
12/31/96					
Net income (loss)					
Dividends					
Issue shares					
12/31/97					
Net income					
Dividends					
12/31/98					

Name________________________________
Class Time___________________________

PROBLEM 2-12 or 2-12A

1.

____________________CORPORATION	
STATEMENT OF CASH FLOWS	
FOR THE YEAR ENDED DECEMBER 31, 1998	
Net cash provided by operating activities:	

2. What does this statement tell you that an income statement doesn't?

Name________________________________

Class Time__________________________

PROBLEM 2-13 or 2-13A

Letter from the President to stockholders of ______________________Inc.:

Name_______________________________
Class Time___________________________

PROBLEM 2-14

1. 1998:
1997:

2.

GLEESON COMPANY	
INCOME STATEMENT	
1997	
Sales	

Name ____________________

Class Time ____________________

PROBLEM 2-14A

1. 1998:
1997:

2. Income statement items as a percentage of sales:		
Sales		
Cost of sales		
Sales salaries		
Delivery expense		
Office supplies		
Depreciation – truck		
Computer line expense		
Total expenses		
Net income		

Why did net income remain unchanged when sales increased?

Calculations:

Name________________________________

Class Time____________________________

PROBLEM 2-15 or 2-15A

1.

____AND SUBSIDIARIES	
____	
YEAR ENDED ______________31, 1995	
Net Sales	

PROBLEM 2-15 or 2-15A continued

2.

________________ AND SUBSIDIARIES
CONSOLIDATED BALANCE SHEET
DECEMBER 31, 1995

Assets

Name________________________________
Class Time___________________________

PROBLEM 2-16 or 2-16A

Cash available to pay a dividend on December 31, 1998:	
Cash balance, ____________________________, 1998	

Calculations:

Conclusions and recommendations:

Name________________________________

Class Time____________________________

EXERCISE 3-1

1.	3.	5.	7.
2.	4.	6.	8.

EXERCISE 3-2

1.	3.	5.	7.
2.	4.	6.	8.

EXERCISE 3-3

Transaction	Assets	Liabilities	Owners' Equity
1.			
2.			
3.			
4.			
5.			
6.			
7.			
8.			
9.			

EXERCISE 3-4

Type of Transaction	Assets	Liabilities	Owners' Equity
1.	Increase	Increase	
2.	Increase		Increase
3.	Decrease	Decrease	
4.	Decrease		Decrease
5.	Increase Decrease		

Name________________________________

Class Time___________________________

EXERCISE 3-7

Correct Entry:		Debit	Credit
Jun 5			

Why is the entry wrong? Why does the bank refer to cash received from a customer as a credit?

EXERCISE 3-8

SPENCER CORPORATION TRIAL BALANCE DECEMBER 31, 1998		
	Debit	Credit
Totals		

Name______________________________
Class Time__________________________

PROBLEM 3-1 or 3-1A

	I or E	Recorded in the accounts? If so, in what accounts?
1.		
2.		
3.		
4.		
5.		
6.		
7.		
8.		
9.*		

* Problem 3-1A has only 8 events.

Name________________________________

Class Time____________________________

PROBLEM 3-3 or 3-3A

1. ____________________________, Inc. Transactions for the month of March1998

Assets					= Liabilities		+ Owners' Equity	
Date	**Cash**	**Accounts Receivable**	**Computer**	**Supplies**	**Accounts Payable**	**Notes Payable**	**Common Stock**	**Retained Earnings**
3/2								
3/7								
Bal.								
3/12								
Bal.								
3/19								
Bal.								
3/20								
Bal.								
3/22								
Bal.								
3/26								
Bal.								
3/29								
Bal.								
3/30								
Bal.								
3/31								
Bal.								

Total Assets: $

Total Liabilities and Owners' Equity: $

Parts 2 and 3 are on the next page.

4. What events do you expect to occur in April?

PROBLEM 3-3 or 3-3A continued

2.

____________________, INC.		
INCOME STATEMENT		
FOR THE MONTH ENDED MARCH 31,1998		
Revenues:		

3.

____________________, INC.		
BALANCE SHEET		
MARCH 31,1998		
Assets		
Liabilities and Owners' Equity		

Name___________________________

Class Time______________________

PROBLEM 3-4

Elm Corporation — Transactions for the month of June1998

	Assets				=	Liabilities		+ Owners' Equity	
Date	**Cash**	**Accounts Rec.**	**Equip.**	**Building**	**Land**	**Accounts Payable**	**Notes Payable**	**Common Stock**	**Retained Earnings**
6/xx									
6/xx									
Bal.									
6/xx									
Bal.									
6/xx									
Bal.									
6/xx									
Bal.									
6/xx									
Bal.									
6/xx									
Bal.									
6/xx									
Bal.									
6/xx									
Bal.									
6/xx									
Bal.									
6/xx									
Bal.									

Total Assets: $

Total Liabilities and Owners' Equity: $

Assumptions:

Name______________________________

Class Time___________________________

PROBLEM 3-4A

Name________________________________

Class Time____________________________

PROBLEM 3-5 or 3-5A

		If recorded		
	Recorded?	1. Source Documents Generated	2. Which Document to Use to Record the Event?	3. Information from Source Document Most Useful in Recording the Event
a.				
b.				
c.				
d.				
e.				
f.				
g.				
h.				

Name________________________________
Class Time__________________________

PROBLEM 3-6 or 3-6A

Transaction	Accounts	
	Debited	Credited
a.		
b.		
c.		
d.		
e.		
f.		
g.		
h.		
I.		
j.		
k.*		

* Problem 3-6 has no “k” transaction.

Name______________________________

Class Time__________________________

PROBLEM 3-7 or 3-7A

Note: Not all accounts will be used by both Problem 3-7 and 3-7A. Problem 3-7 has no transaction for October 9.

1. ______________________________ Transactions for the month of October 1998

Assets							= Liabilities		+ Owners' Equity	
Date	Cash	Accts. Rec.	Conc. Supplies	Land	Building	Equip.	Accts. Payable	Notes Payable	Capital Stock	Retained Earnings
10/1										
Bal.										
10/2										
Bal.										
10/3										
Bal.										
10/9										
Bal.										
10/12										
Bal.										
10/13										
Bal.										
10/17										
Bal.										
10/23										
Bal.										
10/24										
Bal.										
10/26										
Bal.										
10/27										
Bal.										
10/30										
Bal.										
10/31										
Bal.										

Total Assets: $

Total Liabilities and Owners' Equity: $

PROBLEM 3-7 or 3-7A continued

2.

Cash

Accounts Receivable

Concession Supplies

Land

Building

Equipment

Accounts Payable

Note Payable

Capital Stock

Retained Earnings

Name____________________

Class Time____________________

PROBLEM 3-8 or 3-8A

1.

TRIAL BALANCE OCTOBER 31,1998	Debit	Credit

2.

INCOME STATEMENT FOR THE MONTH ENDED OCTOBER 31,1998		
Revenues:		

PROBLEM 3-8 or 3-8A continued

3.

STATEMENT OF RETAINED EARNINGS
FOR THE MONTH ENDED OCTOBER 31,1998

Beginning balance, October 1, 1998	

4.

BALANCE SHEET
OCTOBER 31,1998

Assets		
Liabilities and Owners' Equity		

Name______________________________

Class Time__________________________

PROBLEM 3-9 or 3-9A

		Debit	Credit
a.			
b.			
c.			
d.			
e.			
f.			
g.			
h.			
i.*			

Note: Problem 3-9A has no “i” transaction.

Name______________________________
Class Time__________________________

PROBLEM 3-10 or 3-10A

Note: Not all accounts will be used by both Problem 3-10 and 3-10A.

1.

Cash

Accounts Receivable

Land

Building

Office Equipment

Computer Software

Accounts Payable

Commissions Payable

Unearned Service Revenue

Notes Payable

Capital Stock

______________ Revenue

Wage and Salary Expense

Rent Expense

Commissions Expense

Utilities Expense

PROBLEM 3-10 or 3-10A continued

2.

______________________________		
TRIAL BALANCE		
______________________________**,1998**		
	Debit	Credit

Name______________________________

Class Time__________________________

PROBLEM 3-11

1. Identify the two errors.

2.

MALCOLM, INC.		
REVISED TRIAL BALANCE		
JANUARY 31,1998		
	Debit	Credit

Name____________________________
Class Time________________________

PROBLEM 3-11A

1.

Cash	+	all other debits	=	Total debits

2.

Cash

Explanations:

Name____________________________

Class Time_______________________

PROBLEM 3-12

1.

		Debit	Credit
Jan. 2			
Jan. 3			
Jan. 4			
Jan. 6			
Jan. 31			
Jan. 31			
Jan. 31			

2.

OVERNIGHT DELIVERY, INC.		
TRIAL BALANCE		
JANUARY 31,1998		
	Debit	Credit

3.

OVERNIGHT DELIVERY, INC.		
INCOME STATEMENT		
FOR THE MONTH ENDED JANUARY 31,1998		
Service Revenue		

Name___________________________

Class Time______________________

PROBLEM 3-12 continued

4.

OVERNIGHT DELIVERY, INC. BALANCE SHEET JANUARY 31,1998		
Assets		
Liabilities and Owners' Equity		

5.

Jan. 3

Jan. 4

PROBLEM 3-12 continued

5. continued

Jan. 6
Jan. 31
Jan. 31

Name________________________________
Class Time___________________________

PROBLEM 3-12A

1.

		Debit	Credit
Feb. 2			
Feb. 3			
Feb. 4			
Feb. 15			
Feb. 26			
Feb. 27			

2.
Feb. 2:

Feb. 3:

Feb. 4:

Feb. 27:

Name______________________________

Class Time__________________________

PROBLEM 3-13

1.

		Debit	Credit
Jun. 2			
Jun. 5			
Jun. 8			
Jun. 15			
Jun. 17			
Jun. 23			
Jun. 28			
Jun. 29			
Jun. 30			
Jun. 30			

PROBLEM 3-13 continued

1. continued

		Debit	Credit
Jun. 30			

2.

NEVERANERROR, INC.		
TRIAL BALANCE		
JUNE 30,1998		
	Debit	Credit

3. a.

NEVERANERROR, INC.		
INCOME STATEMENT		
FOR THE MONTH ENDED JUNE 30,1998		
Service Revenue		

Name________________________________

Class Time____________________________

PROBLEM 3-13 continued

3. b.

NEVERANERROR, INC.	
STATEMENT OF RETAINED EARNINGS	
FOR THE MONTH ENDED JUNE 30,1998	
Beginning balance, June 1	

3. c.

NEVERANERROR, INC.		
BALANCE SHEET		
JUNE 30,1998		
Assets		
Liabilities and Owners' Equity		

4. Would you join the company? Explain.

Name________________________________
Class Time____________________________

PROBLEM 3-13A

1.

		Debit	Credit
Jul. 2			
Jul. 3			
Jul. 5			
Jul. 17			
Jul. 28			
Jul. 30			
Jul. 30			
Jul. 31			

PROBLEM 3-13A continued

2.

KRITTERSBEGONE, INC.		
BALANCE SHEET		
JULY 31,1998		
Assets		
Liabilities and Owners' Equity		

What cash inflow and what cash outflow can you predict in the month of August?

Who would be interested in the cash flow information and why?

Name____________________________
Class Time________________________

EXERCISE 4-1

Calculation of amount of revenue to recognize for the year:	

Explanation of how the revenue recognition rule should be applied:

EXERCISE 4-2

	How normally recognized as expense, and explanation if more than one possible
1.	
2.	
3.	
4.	
5.	
6.	
7.	
8.	
9.	

EXERCISE 4-3

	Type of Adjustment		Type of Adjustment		Type of Adjustment
1.		4.		7.	
2.		5.		8.	
3.		6.			

Name________________________________

Class Time____________________________

EXERCISE 4-4

			Debit	Credit
May	31			

Effect on net income if not recorded:

EXERCISE 4-5

1. Rental cost for each full month:

2.

			Debit	Credit
Sep.	1			

3.

			Debit	Credit
Sep.	30			

4. Effect on net income:

Name________________________________
Class Time___________________________

EXERCISE 4-6

1.			Debit	Credit
Jul.	1			

2. Depreciable cost of machine =

3. Monthly depreciation =

4.			Debit	Credit
Jul.	31			

5. Equipment	
Less: Accumulated depreciation	
Carrying value	

EXERCISE 4-7

1. Monthly cost of insurance policy:

2.			Debit	Credit
Apr.	1			

Name________________________________
Class Time____________________________

EXERCISE 4-7 continued

3.			Debit	Credit
Dec.	31			

4. Effect on net income:

EXERCISE 4-8

1.			Debit	Credit
Aug.	xx			

2.			Debit	Credit
Aug.	31			

3. Effect on net income:

EXERCISE 4-9

1.			Debit	Credit
Apr.	1			

Name________________________________
Class Time____________________________

EXERCISE 4-9 continued

2.			Debit	Credit
Apr.	30			

3. Effect on net income:

EXERCISE 4-10

1. Amount of weekly payroll:

2.			Debit	Credit
Oct.	27			

3.			Debit	Credit
Oct.	31			

4.			Debit	Credit
Nov.	3			

5. Effect on net income:

Name________________________________

Class Time____________________________

EXERCISE 4-11

1.			Debit	Credit
Mar.	1			

2.			Debit	Credit
Mar.	31			
Apr.	30			

3.			Debit	Credit
May	30			

EXERCISE 4-12

1. 1998			Debit	Credit
Dec.	31			

2. 1999			Debit	Credit
Jun.	1			

Name______________________________
Class Time__________________________

EXERCISE 4-13

1.			Debit	Credit
Jun.	1			

2.			Debit	Credit
Jun.	30			

3.			Debit	Credit
Jul.	31			

EXERCISE 4-14

1. Recording revenue

2.			Debit	Credit
Jun.	30			

Name________________________________
Class Time____________________________

EXERCISE 4-15

1.		4.	
2.		5.	
3.		6.	

EXERCISE 4-16

	Assets	= Liabilities	+ Owners' Equity
1.			
2.			
3.			
4.			
5.			
6.			

EXERCISE 4-17

1. Adjusting Entries			Debit	Credit
May	31			

Name________________________________
Class Time___________________________

EXERCISE 4-17 continued

1. Adjusting Entries continued			Debit	Credit
May	31			

Net increase(decrease) in net income from adjustments:	

Name______________________________
Class Time__________________________

EXERCISE 4-18

Order of the steps in the accounting cycle:

EXERCISE 4-19

HADLEY REALTY CORPORATION		
ADJUSTED TRIAL BALANCE		
DECEMBER 31		
	Debit	Credit

Name______________________________
Class Time___________________________

EXERCISE 4-20

1. Closing Entries			Debit	Credit
Dec.	31			

2. Net income effect:

EXERCISE 4-21

FISHER CORPORATION	
STATEMENT OF RETAINED EARNINGS	
FOR THE YEAR ENDED DECEMBER 31, 1998	
Beginning balance, January 1, 1998	

Name______________________________

Class Time______________________________

EXERCISE 4-22

Closing Entries			Debit	Credit
Dec.	31			

EXERCISE 4-23

Closing Entries			Debit	Credit
Dec.	31			

Name_______________________________
Class Time___________________________

EXERCISE 4-23 continued

Closing Entries continued			Debit	Credit
Dec.	31			

EXERCISE 4-24

1. Closing Entries			Debit	Credit
Dec.	31			

2. Why are closing entries necessary? When should they be recorded?

Name________________________________
Class Time___________________________

EXERCISE 4-25

Calculation of the balance sheet amount:	

Difference in amounts:

EXERCISE 4-26

Carried to Income Statement (IS) or Balance Sheet (BS) and Normal Balance – Debit (D) or Credit (C)					
1.		6.		11.	
2.		7.		12.	
3.		8.		13.	
4.		9.		14.	
5.		10.		15.	

Name______________________________
Class Time__________________________

EXERCISE 4-30

1.			Debit	Credit
Jul.	1			
Jul.	31			
Aug.	31			

2. Evaluation of statement:

Name______________________________
Class Time__________________________

PROBLEM 4-1 or 4-1A

a.

b.

c.

d.

e.

Name________________________________

Class Time____________________________

PROBLEM 4-3 or 4-3A

Note: Problem 4-3A has no part g.

1.

	Assets	=	Liabilities					+ Owners' Equity	
	Office Supplies	Accum. Depr.	Interest Payable	Wages Payable	Income Tax Payable	Rent Coll. In Advance	Customer Deposits	Capital Stock	Retained Earnings
a.									
b.									
c.									
d.									
e.									
f.									
g.									

2. March net income:	
Unadjusted net income	
Effect of adjustments:	
a.	
b.	
c.	
d.	
e.	
f.	
g.	
Adjusted net income	

Name______________________________

Class Time__________________________

PROBLEM 4-4 or 4-4A

1. Adjusting entries:		Debit	Credit
a.			
b.			
c.			
d.			
e.			
f.			

2. Net increase (decrease) in net income from adjustments:	
a.	
b.	
c.	
d.	
e.	
f.	

Name________________________________
Class Time____________________________

PROBLEM 4-5 or 4-5A

Note: Problem 4-5A has no parts n or o.

	Debit	Credit		Debit	Credit
a.			i.		
b.			j.		
c.			k.		
d.			l.		
e.			m.		
f.			n.		
g.			o.		
h.					

Name______________________________
Class Time__________________________

PROBLEM 4-6 or 4-6A

1. Adjusting entries:			Debit	Credit
Dec.	31			
a.				
b.				
c.				

2. Balance before the adjusting entry is made:

Name____________________________
Class Time________________________

PROBLEM 4-7 or 4-7A

Note: Problem 4-7A has no parts f, g, or h.

1. Adjusting entries:			Debit	Credit
	30			
a.				
b.				
c.				
d.				
e.				
f.				
g.				
h.				

2. Why does Accumulated Depreciation contain a balance?

Name_______________________________
Class Time___________________________

PROBLEM 4-8

1.

	Assets			=	Liabilities		+ Owners' Equity	
	Accounts Rec.	**Office Supplies**	**Prepaid Insurance**	**Accum. Depr.**	**Unearned Commiss-ions**	**Interest Payable**	**Wages Payable**	**Capital Stock**	**Retained Earnings**
a.									
b.									
c.									
d.									
e.									
f.									
g.									
h.									

2. Net increase (decrease) in net income from adjustments:	
a.	
b.	
c.	
d.	
e.	
f.	
g.	
h.	

Name____________________________

Class Time ____________________________

PROBLEM 4-8A

1.

	Assets		=	Liabilities	+	Owners' Equity
	Office Supplies	Prepaid Rent	Accum. Depr.	Interest Payable	Salaries Payable	Capital Stock	Retained Earnings
a.							
b.							
c.							
d.							
e.							

2. Net increase (decrease) in net income from adjustments:	
a.	
b.	
c.	
d.	
e.	

Name ______________________________
Class Time __________________________

PROBLEM 4-9 or 4-9A

1.			Debit	Credit
Jun.	30			

2. Original amount:

3.			Debit	Credit
Jun.	30			

4. Equipment's estimated useful life in months:

5.			Debit	Credit
Jun.	30			

6. Calculation of the monthly interest rate on the loan:

Name______________________________
Class Time__________________________

PROBLEM 4-10

1. and 2.

Cash

Video Inventory

Prepaid Rent

Display Stands

Accumulated Depreciation

Accounts Payable

Wages and Salaries Payable

Income Taxes Payable

Customer Subscriptions

Capital Stock

Retained Earnings

Rental Revenue

Subscription Revenue

Wage and Salary Expense

Utility Expense

Advertising Expense

Rent Expense

Video Expense

Depreciation Expense

Income Tax Expense

Explanations:

(a)

(b)

(c)

1. and 2. continued

(f) Calculation of taxes due:

3. FOUR STAR VIDEO ADJUSTED TRIAL BALANCE MAY 31, 1998	Debit	Credit

4. Does Four Star Video appear to be profitable? Explain.

Name____________________________

Class Time____________________________

PROBLEM 4-10A

1. and 2.

Cash

Accounts Receivable

Prepaid Rent

Chemical Inventory

Equipment

Accumulated Depreciation

Accounts Payable

Wages and Salaries Payable

Income Tax Payable

Capital Stock

Retained Earnings

Treatment Revenue

Wage and Salary Expense

Utility Expense

Advertising Expense

Rent Expense

Depreciation Expense

Chemical Expense

Income Tax Expense

Explanations:

(a)

(b)

(c)

PROBLEM 4-10A continued

1. and 2. continued

(e) Calculation of taxes due:

3.

LEWIS AND ASSOCIATES
ADJUSTED TRIAL BALANCE
JUNE 30, 1998

	Debit	Credit

4. Does Lewis and Associates appear to be profitable? Explain.

Name________________________________

Class Time____________________________

PROBLEM 4-11 and 4-11A

Note: Problem 4-11A has no part f.

1.

	Assets			=	Liabilities		+ Owners' Equity	
	________ Inventory	Prepaid Rent	Accum. Depreciation	Wages & Salary Payable	Taxes Payable	Customer Subscriptions	Capital Stock	Retained Earnings
a.								
b.								
c.								
d.								
e.								
f.								

Explanations:

(a)

(b)

(c)

Calculation of taxes due:	

Name____________________

Class Time____________________

PROBLEM 4-13 or 4-13A

Name________________________________
Class Time____________________________

PROBLEM 4-14 or 4-14A

1. ________________________________

INCOME STATEMENTS

	Year 1	Year 2
Sales revenue		

Explanations:

a. Sales:

b. Advertising expense:

c. ________________________:

d. Rent:

2. Closing entries:			Debit	Credit
Year	1			
Year	2			

Purpose of closing entries:

Name ______________________________

Class Time __________________________

PROBLEM 4-15

1., 2., and 3

ACE CONSULTING, INC.
WORK SHEET
FOR THE MONTH ENDING JUNE 30, 1998

	Unadjusted Trial Balance		Adjusting Entries		Adjusted Trial Balance		Income Statement		Balance Sheet	
Account Titles	**Debit**	**Credit**	**Debit**	**Credit**	**Debit**	**Credit**	**Debit**	**Credit**	**Debit**	**Credit**
Cash										
Accounts Receivable										
Supplies On Hand										
Prepaid Rent										
Furniture & Fixtures										
Accumulated Depreciation										
Accounts Payable										
Capital Stock										
Retained Earnings										
Consulting Revenue										
Utilities Expense										
Wage and Salary Expense										
Wages and Salaries Payable										
Supplies Expense										
Depreciation Expense										
Rent Expense										

Name______________________________
Class Time__________________________

PROBLEM 4-15A

1., 2., and 3

FOREVER GREEN LANDSCAPING WORK SHEET FOR THE MONTH ENDED AUGUST 31, 1998										
	Unadjusted Trial Balance		Adjusting Entries		Adjusted Trial Balance		Income Statement		Balance Sheet	
Account Titles	Debit	Credit	Debit	Credit	Debit	Credit	Debit	Credit	Debit	Credit
Cash										
Accounts Receivable										
Supplies on Hand										
Prepaid Insurance										
Equipment										
Accumulated Depreciation --Equip.										
Building										
Accumulated Depreciation – Build.										
Accounts Payable										
Notes Payable										
Capital Stock										
Retained Earnings										
Service Revenue										
Advertising Expense										
Gasoline and Oil Expense										
Wage and Salary Expense										
Supplies Expense										
Insurance Expense										
Depreciation Expense – Equip.										
Depreciation Expense -- Building										
Rent Receivable										
Rent Revenue										
Wages And Salaries Payable										
Interest Expense										
Interest Payable										

Name________________________________

Class Time____________________________

PROBLEM 4-15A continued

Explanation for adjusting entry amounts:

(a)

(b)

(c)

(d)

(g)

4. Closing entries:			Debit	Credit
Aug.	31			

Name____________________

Class Time____________________

PROBLEM 4-16

1.			Debit	Credit
Jan.	2			
Jan.	2			
Jan.	3			
Jan.	4			
Jan.	5			
Jan.	6			
Jan.	7			
Jan.	15			
Jan.	16			
Jan.	31			

PROBLEM 4-16 continued

1. continued			Debit	Credit
Jan.	31			
Jan.	31			

2.

Cash

Land

House

Furniture

Prepaid Insurance

Cleaning Supplies

Accounts Payable

Rent Received in Advance

Notes Payable

Capital Stock

Dividends

Revenue from Rental of Rooms

Restaurant Revenue

Advertising Expense

Wages Expense

Name________________________________
Class Time____________________________

PROBLEM 4-16 continued

3., 4., and 5.

MOONLIGHT BAY INN
WORK SHEET
FOR THE MONTH ENDING JANUARY 31, 1998

	Unadjusted Trial Balance		Adjusting Entries		Adjusted Trial Balance		Income Statement		Balance Sheet	
Account Titles	Debit	Credit	Debit	Credit	Debit	Credit	Debit	Credit	Debit	Credit
Cash										
Land										
House										
Accumulated Depreciation–House										
Furniture										
Accumulated Depreciation –Furn.										
Prepaid Insurance										
Cleaning Supplies										
Accounts Payable										
Notes Payable										
Rent Received in Advance										
Capital Stock										
Advertising Expense										
Wages Expense										
Revenue from Rental of Rooms										
Restaurant Revenue										
Dividends										
Depreciation Expense – House										
Depreciation Expense -- Furniture										
Interest Expense										
Interest Payable										
Insurance Expense										
Wages Payable										
Supplies Expense										
Utilities Expense										
Utilities Payable										
Income Tax Expense										
Income Tax Payable										

PROBLEM 4-16 continued

3., 4., and 5

Explanations:
(a)
(b)
(c)
(d)
(e)
(f)
(g)
(h)
(i) Calculation of tax expense:

6.a. MOONLIGHT BAY INN INCOME STATEMENT FOR THE MONTH ENDED JANUARY 31, 1998		
Revenues:		

Name____________________________
Class Time________________________

PROBLEM 4-16 continued

6. b.	MOONLIGHT BAY INN
	STATEMENT OF RETAINED EARNINGS
	FOR THE MONTH ENDED JANUARY 31, 1998
Beginning balance, January 1, 1998	

6. c.	MOONLIGHT BAY INN		
	BALANCE SHEET		
	JANUARY 31, 1998		
Assets			
Liabilities			

6. c. Balance Sheet continued			
Stockholders' equity			

7. What are your reactions to the first month of operations? Are you comfortable with the loan you made?

Name________________________________

Class Time____________________________

PROBLEM 4-16A

1., 2., and 3

TENFOUR TRUCKING COMPANY
WORK SHEET
FOR THE MONTH ENDING JANUARY 31, 1998

	Unadjusted Trial Balance		Adjusting Entries		Adjusted Trial Balance		Income Statement		Balance Sheet	
Account Titles	**Debit**	**Credit**	**Debit**	**Credit**	**Debit**	**Credit**	**Debit**	**Credit**	**Debit**	**Credit**
Cash										
Accounts Receivable										
Prepaid Insurance										
Warehouse										
Accumulated Depreciation—Warehouse										
Truck Fleet										
Accumulated Depreciation—Truck Fleet										
Land										
Accounts Payable										
Notes Payable										
Interest Payable										
Customer Deposit										
Capital Stock										
Retained Earnings										
Freight Revenue										
Gasoline and Oil Expense										
Maintenance Expense										
Wage and Salary Expense										
Dividends Declared and Paid										
Insurance Expense										
Depreciation Expense-Warehouse										
Depreciation Expense-Truck Fleet										
Interest Expense										
Wages and Salaries Payable										
Income Tax Expense										
Income Tax Payable										

PROBLEM 4-16A continued

Explanations:
(a)
(b)
(c)
(d)
(e)
(f)
(g) Calculation of tax expense:

4.a	TENFOUR TRUCKING COMPANY	
	INCOME STATEMENT	
	FOR THE MONTH ENDED JANUARY 31, 1998	
Freight revenue		

Name________________________________

Class Time____________________________

PROBLEM 4-16A continued

4. b. TENFOUR TRUCKING COMPANY	
STATEMENT OF RETAINED EARNINGS	
FOR THE MONTH ENDED JANUARY 31, 1998	
Beginning balance, January 1, 1998	

4. c. TENFOUR TRUCKING COMPANY			
BALANCE SHEET			
JANUARY 31, 1998			
Assets			
Liabilities			
Stockholders' Equity			

PROBLEM 4-16A continued

5. Current ratio =

What does this ratio tell you about this company's liquidity?

6. Why is it not possible to compute a gross profit ratio? Describe a meaningful measure of profitability.

Name________________________________
Class Time__________________________

EXERCISE 5-1

March 3			Debit	Credit
a.				
b.				
c.				
d.				
e.				

EXERCISE 5-2

Terms	Last Day of Payment	Amount to Pay with Discount	Date Full Payment Due
a. 2/10, n/30			
b. 3/15, n/45			
c. 1/7, n/21			
d. 5/15, n/30			

Name________________________________

Class Time____________________________

EXERCISE 5-3

			Debit	Credit
Jun.	2			
Jun.	4			
Jun.	13			
Jun.	30			

EXERCISE 5-4

1. Would L. A. Gear still be considered a merchandiser?

2.	1995	1994

Name____________________
Class Time____________________

EXERCISE 5-4 continued

2. **Estimated Cost of Sales**	
1994	
1995	

EXERCISE 5-5

Merchandiser	**Inventory System**
Appliance store	
Car dealership	
Drug store	
Furniture store	
Grocery store	
Hardware store	
Jewelry store	

Changes in technology affecting perpetual inventory:

Name______________________________
Class Time__________________________

EXERCISE 5-6

	Case 1	Case 2	Case 3
Beginning inventory	$	$2,350	$1,890
Purchases (gross)	6,230	5,720	
Purchase returns and allowances	470	800	550
Purchase discounts	200		310
Transportation-in	150	500	420
Cost of goods available for sale	7,110		8,790
Ending inventory		1,750	1,200
Cost of goods sold	5,220	5,570	

Calculations:

EXERCISE 5-7

			Debit	Credit
Jul.	3			
Jul.	6			
Jul.	12			
Aug.	5			

Name______________________________

Class Time__________________________

EXERCISE 5-8

			Debit	Credit
Mar.	3			
Mar.	3			
Mar.	7			
Mar.	12			
Mar.	15			
Mar.	18			
Mar.	22			
Apr.	6			
Apr.	18			

Name________________________________
Class Time ____________________________

EXERCISE 5-10

In Transit from Vendors:	**Month Recorded**
Shipped FOB shipping point	
Shipped FOB destination point	
In Transit from Customers:	
Shipped FOB shipping point	
Shipped FOB destination	

EXERCISE 5-12

Task	**Employee**		
	Mary	**Sue**	**John**
Prepare invoices			
Mail invoices			
Pick up mail from post office			
Open mail, separate checks			
List checks on deposit slip in triplicate			
Post payments to customer's account			
Deposit checks			
Prepare monthly schedule of accounts receivable			
Reconcile bank statements			

EXERCISE 5-13

Missing Amounts	**Solution**
a. Sales return and allowances	
b. Purchases	
c. Net purchases	
d. Cost of goods sold	
e. Ending inventory	
f. Operating expenses	
g. Net income	

Name________________________________

Class Time____________________________

EXERCISE 5-14

LAPINE COMPANY INCOME STATEMENT FOR THE YEAR ENDED DECEMBER 31, 1998			
Sales			

2. Calculation of gross margin ratio:	

Name________________________________
Class Time___________________________

PROBLEM 5-1 or 5-1A

1. Explanation of discounts:

2. Comments and explanations:

Name________________________________

Class Time___________________________

PROBLEM 5-2 or 5-2A

1.	1995		1994	
(in millions)	**Sales**	**Cost of Sales**	**Sales**	**Cost of Sales**

2. Which company appears to be performing better? What factors might cause the difference? Other information needed?

Name____________________________

Class Time________________________

PROBLEM 5-3 or 5-3A

Note: Problem 5-3A has no part 3.

1.

2.

3.

Name

Class Time

PROBLEM 5-4 or 5-4A

1.

2.

Name______________________________
Class Time__________________________

PROBLEM 5-5 or 5-5A

Note: Problem 5-5A has no transaction on the 22nd.

1.			Debit	Credit
	2			
	4			
	5			
	6			
	7			
	11			
	13			
	22			
	30			

PROBLEM 5-5 or 5-5A continued

2.

Name______________________________

Class Time__________________________

PROBLEM 5-6 or 5-6A

1.			Debit	Credit
Apr.	3			
Apr.	7			
Apr.	8			
Apr.	9			
Apr.	10			
Apr.	13			
Apr.	17			
Apr.	20			

2. Change to a perpetual system? Why? Advantages?

Name________________________________

Class Time____________________________

PROBLEM 5-7 or 5-7A

1. Sale and receipt			Debit	Credit
Sep.	12			
Sep.	21			

2. Purchase and payment			Debit	Credit
Sep.	12			
Sep.	21			

Name________________________________
Class Time___________________________

PROBLEM 5-8 or 5-8A

Note: Problem 5-8A has no part f or g.

1.			Debit	Credit
a.				
b.				
c.				
d.				
e.				
f.				
g.				

PROBLEM 5-8 or 5-8A continued

2. ______________________________, INC.

PARTIAL INCOME STATEMENT

FOR THE MONTH ENDED _____________, 1998

Sales revenue			

3.

Name________________________________
Class Time____________________________

PROBLEM 5-9 or 5-9A

1.			Debit	Credit
	1			
	10			
	15			
	18			
	25			
	—			

2.

PROBLEM 5-9 or 5-9A continued

2. continued

3.

4.

Name______________________________
Class Time__________________________

PROBLEM 5-10

1. Why doesn't The Gap's balance sheet include accounts receivable?

2. Sales for the year			Debit	Credit
Feb.	3			

3. Deductions to arrive at net sales and reasons why not reported separately:

4. Cost of goods sold section:

5. Gross margin (gross profit) ratios:

($000)	**1996**	**1995**	**1994**
Sales			

PROBLEM 5-10 continued

Comments on changes in gross margin; evaluation of performance; and the factors causing the change:

Name______________________________
Class Time__________________________

PROBLEM 5-10A

1.			Debit	Credit
Feb.	3			
Feb.	3			
Feb.	3			

2. Deductions to arrive at net sales and reasons why not reported separately

3. Cost of goods sold section:

4. Gross margin ratios:	1996	1995

PROBLEM 5-10A continued

Is the Company's performance improving? What factors are causing the change?

Name______________________________

Class Time____________________________

PROBLEM 5-11 or 5-11A

1. Problems:

2. Suggestions:

3. Explanation of lack of personal responsibility:

Name______________________________
Class Time__________________________

PROBLEM 5-12 or 5-12A

1. Cost of Goods Sold for 1998:

2. Net income for 1998

PROBLEM 5-12 or 5-12A continued

BALANCE SHEET
AT DECEMBER 31, 1998

Assets:

Liabilities:

Stockholders' Equity:

Name______________________________

Class Time____________________________

EXERCISE 6-1

Inventory Item	Raw Material	Work in Process	Finished Goods	Merchandise Inventory
Fabric				
Lumber				
Unvarnished tables				
Chairs on the floor				
Cushions				
Decorative knobs				
Drawers				
Sofa frames				
Chairs in warehouse				
Chairs in storeroom				

EXERCISE 6-2

Inventoriable Costs:	

Explain all items not included in inventory:

Name________________________________
Class Time____________________________

EXERCISE 6-3

Effect on net income and actions if you were the accountant:

EXERCISE 6-4

	Inventory	Retained Earnings	Cost of Goods Sold	Net Income
1.				
2.				
3.				
4.				

EXERCISE 6-5

1.
2.
3.
4.

Name________________________________
Class Time___________________________

EXERCISE 6-5 continued

5.

6.

EXERCISE 6-6

1. **Ending inventory**		**Cost of goods sold**	

2. **Ending inventory**		**Cost of goods sold**	

3. **Ending inventory**		**Cost of goods sold**	

Name____________________________

Class Time________________________

EXERCISE 6-6 continued

4. **Cost of goods available for sale and units available:**	

Weighted average cost::
Ending Inventory:
Cost of goods sold:

EXERCISE 6-7

	Method		**Method**
1.		5.	
2.		6.	
3.		7.	
4.		8.	

EXERCISE 6-8

1.

Name________________________________
Class Time____________________________

EXERCISE 6-8 continued

2.

EXERCISE 6-9

Calculations:

1.

2.

3.

Journal entry:

Name________________________________
Class Time____________________________

EXERCISE 6-11

Transaction	Effect on Cash Flows
Increase in accounts payable	
Decrease in accounts payable	
Increase in inventories	
Decrease in inventories	

EXERCISE 6-12

Cash payments for inventory:	

EXERCISE 6-13

Cash flows from operating activities:	

Name________________________________
Class Time____________________________

EXERCISE 6-14

	Periodic	Dr.	Cr.	Perpetual	Dr.	Cr.
Oct. 1						
Oct. 3						
Oct. 8						
Oct. 20						

EXERCISE 6-15

1. a. Cost of goods available for sale and units available:

Name______________________________
Class Time____________________________

EXERCISE 6-15 continued

b. **FIFO**

Ending inventory		**Cost of goods sold**	

c. **LIFO**

Ending inventory		**Cost of goods sold**	

2. Effect on taxes using FIFO instead of LIFO:

Name____________________
Class Time____________________

EXERCISE 6-17

1. a. Moving Average

Date	Purchases			Sales			Balance		
	Units	Unit Cost	Total Cost	Units	Unit Cost	Total Cost	Units	Unit Cost	Balance
1/1									
2/12									
3/5									
4/30									
6/12									
7/7									
8/23									
9/6									
10/2									
12/3									

Computations:

Name________________________________
Class Time__________________________

EXERCISE 6-17 continued

1. b. FIFO

Date	Purchases			Sales			Balance		
	Units	Unit Cost	Total Cost	Units	Unit Cost	Total Cost	Units	Unit Cost	Balance
1/1									
2/12									
3/5									
4/30									
6/12									
7/7									
8/23									
9/6									
10/2									
12/3									

Computations:

Name____________________________
Class Time__________________________

EXERCISE 6-17 continued

1. c. LIFO

Date	Purchases			Sales			Balance		
	Units	Unit Cost	Total Cost	Units	Unit Cost	Total Cost	Units	Unit Cost	Balance
1/1									
2/12									
3/5									
4/30									
6/12									
7/7									
8/23									
9/6									
10/2									
12/3									

Computations:

Name________________________________
Class Time____________________________

EXERCISE 6-17 continued

2.	Exercise 6-15		Exercise 6-17		Compare
	EI	CGS	EI	CGS	
Average Cost					
FIFO					
LIFO					

3. Cost of goods sold:

Conclusion:

Name______________________________
Class Time__________________________

PROBLEM 6-1

Business	Types of Costs	Accounting Treatment		
		Expense	**Inventory**	**Other**
Retail shoe store	Shoes for sale			
	Shoe boxes			
	Advertising signs			
Grocery store	Canned goods on the shelves			
	Produce			
	Cleaning supplies			
	Cash registers			
Frame shop	Wooden frame supplies			
	Nails			
	Glass			
Walk-in print shop	Paper			
	Copy machines			
	Toner cartridges			
Restaurant	Frozen food			
	China and silverware			
	Prepared food			
	Spices			

Name________________________________
Class Time____________________________

PROBLEM 6-1A

1.

2.

Name____________________

Class Time____________________

PROBLEM 6-2 or 6-2A

Note: Problem 6-2 has no part 4.

1. Revised income statements	**1998**	**1997**

Revised balance sheets	**12/31/98**	**12/31/97**

2.

PROBLEM 6-2 or 6-2A continued

3.

4.

Name____________________________
Class Time__________________________

PROBLEM 6-3 or 6-3A

Note: Problem 6-3A has no part 3 or 4.

1.

2.

3.

PROBLEM 6-3 or 6-3A continued

4.

Name________________________________

Class Time____________________________

PROBLEM 6-4 or 6-4A

1. (1) Cost of goods available for sale:		

(2) Cost of goods sold:		

(3) Inventory at time of explosion:		

(4) Inventory saved:		

(5) Inventory lost in explosion:		

2.			Debit	Credit
Aug.	1			

Name________________________________
Class Time____________________________

PROBLEM 6-5

1. Gross margin ratios:

(in millions)	Compaq Computer 1995	Compaq Computer 1994	Digital Equipment 1996	Digital Equipment 1995

Company		Ratio
Compaq Computer:		
Digital Equipment:		

PROBLEM 6-5 continued

3. Which company appears to be performing better? Other information needed?

Name____________________________
Class Time________________________

PROBLEM 6-5A

Company	Ratio
Walmart:	
Kmart:	

2. Which company appears to be performing better? Any other information needed?

Name________________________________
Class Time____________________________

PROBLEM 6-6 or 6-6A

1. ____________________

STATEMENT OF CASH FLOWS

FOR THE YEAR ENDED DECEMBER 31, 1998

2. Memorandum to the president:

To: President of ________________

From:

Date:

Subject:

Name________________________________

Class Time___________________________

PROBLEM 6-7 or 6-7A

1.	Cost of goods sold	Ending Inventory	Total
a. Weighted average			
b. FIFO			
c. LIFO			

a.	Calculations	Amount
Beginning inventory		
Oct. 8		
Oct. 18		
Oct. 29		

Calculations:

b. **Ending inventory-FIFO**		**Cost of goods sold-FIFO**	

c. **Ending inventory-LIFO**		**Cost of goods sold-LIFO**	

PROBLEM 6-7 or 6-7A continued

2. What does this column represent?

3. Income statements:

	Weighted Average	FIFO	LIFO

4. Additional taxes using FIFO

Name________________________________

Class Time____________________________

PROBLEM 6-8 or 6-8A

1.	Cost of Goods Sold	Ending Inventory	Total
a. Moving average			
b. FIFO			
c. LIFO			

1. a. Moving Average

Date	Purchases			Sales			Balance		
	Units	Unit Cost	Total Cost	Units	Unit Cost	Total Cost	Units	Unit Cost	Balance

Calculations:

PROBLEM 6-8 or 6-8A continued

1. b. FIFO

Date	Purchases			Sales			Balance		
	Units	Unit Cost	Total Cost	Units	Unit Cost	Total Cost	Units	Unit Cost	Balance

1. c. LIFO

Date	Purchases			Sales			Balance		
	Units	Unit Cost	Total Cost	Units	Unit Cost	Total Cost	Units	Unit Cost	Balance

2.

Name________________________________

Class Time____________________________

PROBLEM 6-8 or 6-8A continued

3. Income statements:

	Moving Average	FIFO	LIFO

4. Additional taxes using FIFO:

Name________________________________

Class Time____________________________

PROBLEM 6-9 or 6-9A

1. Calculation of Units:

	Ending Inventory	Cost of Goods Sold	Total
a. Weighted average			
b. FIFO			
c. LIFO			

a. **Ending inventory - FIFO**		**Cost of goods sold - FIFO**	

b. **Ending inventory - LIFO**		**Cost of goods sold - LIFO**	

c. **Weighted average**	
Beginning inventory	
Nov. 4	
Nov. 13	
Nov. 18	
Nov. 24	

Calculations:

2. Calculation of gross margin and net income:

	FIFO	LIFO	Weighted Average
Sales			

3. Under which method will taxes be the least?

Name____________________________
Class Time______________________

PROBLEM 6-10 or 6-10A

1. a. **Weighted average**

Beginning inventory

Calculations:

b. **Ending inventory - FIFO** **Cost of goods sold - FIFO**

c. **Ending inventory - LIFO** **Cost of goods sold - LIFO**

PROBLEM 6-10 or 6-10A continued

2. Income Statement for the year end December 31, 1998:

	Weighted Average	FIFO	LIFO
Sales			

3.

4.

Name______________________________
Class Time___________________________

PROBLEM 6-11 or 6-11A

1.

2.

Name____________________
Class Time__________________

PROBLEM 6-12 or 6-12A

1.

2.

Name________________________________

Class Time___________________________

EXERCISE 7-10

Change in Balance	Added To or Subtracted From Net Income
Increase in accounts receivable	
Decrease in accounts receivable	
Increase in notes receivable	
Decrease in notes receivable	

EXERCISE 7-11

Cash collections from operating activities:	

EXERCISE 7-12

Included in Cash and Cash Equivalents? Yes (Y) or No (N) If not, where?			
1.		7.	
2.		8.	
3.		9.	
4.		10.	
5.		11.	
6.			

EXERCISE 7-13

Classification: Cash Equivalent (CE), Short-term Investment (STI), or Long-term Investment (LTI)									
1.		3.		5.		7.		9.	
2.		4.		6.		8.		10.	

Name______________________________
Class Time__________________________

EXERCISE 7-14

Cash equivalents at December 31, 1998:	

EXERCISE 7-15

Item	Type of Cash Flow Activity
Purchase of cash equivalents	
Redemption of cash equivalents	
Purchase of short-term investments	
Sale of short-term investments	
Replenishment of the petty cash fund	
Write-off customer account (under the allowance method)	

Name____________________

Class Time____________________

PROBLEM 7-1

1. CALICO CORNERS BANK RECONCILIATION MAY 31, 1998		
Balance per bank statement, May 31		
Add:		
Less:		
Adjusted balance, May 31		
Balance per books, May 31		
Adjusted balance, May 31		

2. 1998			Debit	Credit
May	31			
May	31			
May	31			
May	31			
May	31			

PROBLEM 7-1 continued

3. Explanation to your friend:

Name________________________________
Class Time___________________________

PROBLEM 7-1A

1. KAREN'S CATERING BANK RECONCILIATION MARCH 31, 1998		
Balance per bank statement, March 31		
Add:		
Less:		
Adjusted balance, March 31		
Balance per books, March 31		
Adjusted balance, March 31		

2. Recommendation to Karen:

Name______________________________

Class Time__________________________

PROBLEM 7-2 or 7-2A

1. Journal entry to establish fund:			Debit	Credit

Is the amount appropriate? Explain.

2. Journal entry at the end of the month:			Debit	Credit

What is the effect on total assets? On income?

3.

Name________________________________
Class Time____________________________

PROBLEM 7-3 or 7-3A

1. Summary journal entries:			Debit	Credit
Dec.	31			
Dec.	31			
Dec.	31			

2. a. Bad debt expense at 3% of credit sales:			Debit	Credit
2. b. Bad debt expense at 6% of accounts receivable:				

3. a. **Calculation Of Net Realizable Value Under (a):**	

PROBLEM 7-3 or 7-3A continued

3. b. **Calculation of Net Realizable Value Under (b):**

4. Effect of recognition of bad debt expense on net realizable value:

Effect of write-off on net realizable value:

Name______________________________
Class Time__________________________

PROBLEM 7-4

1. Category	Amount	Estimated Percent Uncollectible	Estimated Amount Uncollectible
Current			
Past due:			
Less than 1 month			
1 to 2 months			
More than 2 months			
Totals			

2. 1998			Debit	Credit
Dec.	31			

3. **Partial balance sheet at December 31, 1998**		

Name______________________________
Class Time ____________________________

PROBLEM 7-4A

1. Category	Amount	Estimated Percent Uncollectible	Estimated Amount Uncollectible
Current			
Past due:			
Less than 1 month			
1 to 2 months			
More than 2 months			
Totals			

2. How would you handle this situation?

3. Partial balance sheet at December 31, 1998		

Name______________________________
Class Time______________________________

PROBLEM 7-5 or 7-5A

Calculations	**Company**	
	__________	__________
1. Accounts receivable turnover		
2. Average collection period		

Comments on the reasonableness of the collection period:

3. Which company appears to be performing better? Other information needed?

Name________________________________

Class Time____________________________

PROBLEM 7-6

1. a. 1998			Debit	Credit
May	31			
1. b.				
Jun.	30			
1. c.				
Aug.	29			

2. **Computation of Effective Rate of Interest:**

Explanation of part 2 answer:

Name ____________________

Class Time ____________________

PROBLEM 7-6A

1. 1998			Debit	Credit
Aug.	29			

2. **Calculation of Effective Rate of Interest:**

Explanation of part 2 answer:

Name______________________________
Class Time______________________________

PROBLEM 7-7 or 7-7A

1. Calculation:

2.

Name____________________________
Class Time________________________

PROBLEM 7-8 or 7-8A

1. ____________________________

STATEMENT OF CASH FLOWS
FOR THE YEAR ENDED DECEMBER 31, 1998

Net income/loss		

2. Memorandum to the president:

To: Owner of ______________________
From:
Date: January XX, 1999
Subject: Cash Flows

Name________________________________
Class Time____________________________

PROBLEM 7-10 or 7-10A

1. 1998			Debit	Credit

2. Comments on partial payment and signing of note for balance:

Name____________________
Class Time____________________

PROBLEM 8-2 or 8-2A

Note: Problem 8-2A has no part 3.

1. Calculation of relative fair value:

		Asset 1	Asset 2	Asset 3
a.				
b.				
c.				

2. Effect of purchase:

3.

Name______________________________
Class Time__________________________

PROBLEM 8-3 or 8-3A

Income Taxes to be Paid If Asset is Not Purchased:

Income Taxes to be Paid If Asset is Purchased:				
Year	**Income before Tax and Depreciation**	**Depreciation Expense**	**Income Before Tax**	**Income Taxes**
1998				
1999				
2000				
2001				
2002				

Amount of Depreciation Tax Shield:

Name____________________________
Class Time__________________________

PROBLEM 8-4 or 8-4A

1.

Year	Straight-line	MACRS	Difference
1			
2			
3			
4			
5			
6			

2. Memorandum to the president:

To: President

From:

Date:

Subject:

Name______________________________
Class Time__________________________

PROBLEM 8-5

1. **OHARE COMPANY**
INCOME STATEMENT
FOR THE YEAR ENDED DECEMBER 31, 1998

2. Calculation of amount of net cash inflow for 1998:

3. Explanation of why net income is not equal to net cash inflow:

4. What amount would appear in cash flow from operating activities?

Name____________________________

Class Time____________________________

PROBLEM 8-5A

1. Calculation of income Book will report in 1998:

2. Calculation of cash on hand at December 31, 1998:

3. Explanation of cash increase:

Why does the increase in cash not equal the income?

Name______________________________
Class Time____________________________

PROBLEM 8-6 or 8-6A

1. Book value of ______________ at time of sale:

Book value of ______________ at time of sale:

2. Calculation of book value of net property, plant and equipment at December 31, 1997:

3. Calculation of net book value of intangibles at December 31, 1997:

Name____________________________

Class Time________________________

PROBLEM 8-7

1. Value assigned to each asset:

a.

b.

c.

d.

2. Amount of 1998 depreciation:

a.

b.

c.

d.

3. Balance sheet presentation at December 31, 1998:

Name________________________________

Class Time__________________________

PROBLEM 8-7A

Depreciation or amortization amount for each asset and book value:
a. Depreciation:
Book value:
b. Depreciation:
Book value:
c. Depreciation:
Book value:
d. Amortization:
Book value:

Name______________________________
Class Time___________________________

PROBLEM 8-7A continued

2. Balance sheet presentation at December 31, 1998:		

Name______________________________
Class Time____________________________

PROBLEM 8-8

1. Amount of depreciation for equipment in year 1:
What do you believe is the correct amount of depreciation to report?
2. Income that will be reported in year 1:
Income that should be reported in year 1:
3. Difference between a cost and an expense:

Name____________________________
Class Time____________________________

PROBLEM 8-8A

1. Is the amount correct? If not, explain how each expenditure should be recorded:

2. Depreciation on income statement in year 1:

How much should have been reported?

3. Amount of income reported:

Correct amount of income:

4. Explanation of amount to capitalize:

Effect on income statement and balance sheet:

Name______________________________

Class Time__________________________

PROBLEM 8-9 or 8-9A

1. Amount of depreciation for 1997:

Amount of depreciation for 1998:

2. Explanation of why the cost was not expensed:

Conditions necessary to allow expensing:

Preference:

3. Amount of gain or loss when sold:

Amount of gain or loss if expensed:

Name______________________________
Class Time___________________________

PROBLEM 8-10

1. Recording of costs:

2. Calculation of amortization expense per year through 1998:

3. Calculation of amortization expense for 1999:

Name______________________________

Class Time__________________________

PROBLEM 8-10A

1. Amount of goodwill:

Calculation of amortization expense for 1998:

2. Calculation of amortization expense for 1999:

Name__________________________________
Class Time________________________________

PROBLEM 8-11 or 8-11A

1. Partial statement of cash flows for 1998:

Partial statement of cash flows for 1999:

Calculations:

2. Why sell at a loss and purchase new equipment?

Name_______________________________

Class Time_________________________

PROBLEM 8-12 or 8-12A

1. Calculation of amortization expense for 1998:

2. Calculation of acquisition cost:

Calculation of when it was acquired:

Calculation of estimated useful life:

How is the acquisition cost reported on the statement of cash flows?

3. How is amortization reported on the statement of cash flows?

4. How is the sale reported on the statement of cash flows?

Name______________________________
Class Time__________________________

EXERCISE 9-1

Accounts	**Current Liability? If Not, What Balance Sheet Category?**
Taxes Payable	
Accounts Receivable	
Notes Payable, 9%, due In 90 days	
Investment In Bonds	
Capital Stock	
Accounts Payable	
Estimated Warranty Payable In 1999	
Retained Earnings	
Trademark	
Mortgage Payable	

EXERCISE 9-2

1. and 2.

	Classification	**Account Title**
a.		
b.		
c.		
d.		
e.		
f.		
g.		

3. Investors and creditors interest in whether a current or long-term liability:

Name________________________________
Class Time____________________________

EXERCISE 9-3

JACKIE COMPANY BALANCE SHEET DECEMBER 31, 1998		
Current liabilities:		

EXERCISE 9-4

1.			Debit	Credit
a.				
b.				
c.				
d.				
e.				

Name________________________________
Class Time____________________________

EXERCISE 9-11

Change in Account Balance	Reported as Operating (O); Investing (I); Financing (F); or Not Separately Reported on SCF (N)
Accrued vacation days	
Health insurance premiums payable	
FICA payable	
Union dues payable	
Salary payable	
Unemployment taxes payable	

EXERCISE 9-12

1998			Debit	Credit

Calculation of Estimated Liability for Warranties account balance:	
Beginning balance	$ 120000

Name______________________________

Class Time___________________________

EXERCISE 9-13

Part 1. Calculation of simple interest:
1.
2.
3.

Part 2. Calculation of interest compounded annually:
1. n=6, 4%
2. n=4, 6%
3. n=3, 8%

Part 3. Calculation of interest compounded semiannually:
1. n=12, 2%
2. n=8, 3%
3. n=6, 4%

Conclusions from comparison:

Name____________________________
Class Time________________________

EXERCISE 9-14

Calculation of amount Brian must deposit now:

EXERCISE 9-15

(a) Interest compounded annually:
(b) Interest compounded semiannually:
(c) Interest compounded quarterly:

EXERCISE 9-16

1. (a) Interest compounded annually:
(b) Interest compounded semiannually:
(c) Interest compounded quarterly:
2. (a) Interest compounded annually:
(b) Interest compounded semiannually:
(c) Interest compounded quarterly:

Name________________________________

Class Time____________________________

EXERCISE 9-17

1. (a) Interest compounded annually:
(b) Interest compounded semiannually:
(c) Interest compounded quarterly:
2. (a) Interest compounded annually:
(b) Interest compounded semiannually:
(c) Interest compounded quarterly:

EXERCISE 9-18

Calculation of amount in bank:

EXERCISE 9-19

Calculation of years to accumulate $41,000:

EXERCISE 9-20

1. Calculation of value of car:
2. Calculation of quarterly payment amount:

Name________________________________
Class Time____________________________

EXERCISE 9-20 continued

2. continued. Calculation of difference in interest:	
With annual payments:	
With quarterly payments:	
Calculation of interest saved:	
Effect on payment and interest if monthly payments:	

EXERCISE 9-21

1. 1998			Debit	Credit
Jan.	31			
2.				
Jan.	31			

Name________________________________
Class Time____________________________

EXERCISE 9-21 continued

3. How would fringe benefits affect payroll entries?

EXERCISE 9-22

1. Employee	Tax Type	Calculations	Employer's Payroll Taxes
Dell			
Fin			
Hook			
Patty			
Tuss			
Woo			

2. 1998			Debit	Credit

Name________________________________
Class Time____________________________

EXERCISE 9-23

			Debit	Credit
(a)				
(b)				

Should the owner offer cumulative vacation and sick pay?

EXERCISE 9-24

Option 1:
Option 2:
Option 3:
Option 4:
Which option should Jane choose?

EXERCISE 9-25

1. Calculation of interest rate:
2. Calculation of money available:

Name______________________________
Class Time__________________________

PROBLEM 9-1 or 9-1A

1a.			Debit	Credit
Jan.	1			
b.				
Jan.	10			
c.				
Feb.	1			
d.				
Mar.	1			
e.				
Jun.	1			
f.				
Jun.	30			

PROBLEM 9-1 or 9-1A

1g.			Debit	Credit
Aug.	1			
h.				
Sep.	1			
i.				
Nov.	1			
j.				
Dec.	31			

2. Outstanding notes:

Amount of interest due:

Name____________________________

Class Time____________________________

PROBLEM 9-2 or 9-2A

1. Adjustments to reconcile net income to net cash provided by operating activities:

Explanation of items not included:

2. Decision of ability to pay when bills become due:

Name________________________________

Class Time____________________________

PROBLEM 9-3 or 9-3A

1. Adjustments to reconcile net income to net cash provided by operating activities:		

2. Explanation of items not included:

Name________________________________
Class Time___________________________

PROBLEM 9-4 or 9-4A

1. Calculation of ending current liability balances:	

2. Types of liabilities included:

3. Decision of ability to pay when bills become due:

Name______________________________

Class Time__________________________

PROBLEM 9-5 or 9-5A

Note: Problem 9-5A has no part 3. If you are assigned Problem 9-5A, your instructor may ask you to complete part 3 of Problem 9-5 using the data from Problem 9-5A.

1. **Defective units needed for repair**	
2. **Percentage to be returned**	

3. Steps necessary if actual warranty costs are significantly higher than the estimated liability recorded at the end of 1998:

Name________________________________
Class Time____________________________

PROBLEM 9-6 or 9-6A

Note: Problem 9-6 has no part 3.

			Debit	Credit
1.				
2.				

3. Calculation of Estimated Liability for Warranties account balance:	
Beginning balance	$ 1100

Name______________________________

Class Time__________________________

PROBLEM 9-7

1. 1998			Debit	Credit
Dec.	31			
1999				
Dec.	31			
2000				
Jun.	30			

2. 1998			Debit	Credit
Dec.	31			
1999				
Dec.	31			
2000				
Jun.	30			

3. Computation of additional interest:	

Name______________________________

Class Time__________________________

PROBLEM 9-7A

1. **Computation of simple interest:**	
December 31, 1998:	
December 31, 1999	
June 30, 2000	

2. **Computation of compound interest:**		
December 31, 1998:		
December 31, 1999:		
June 30, 2000:		
Total accrued		

3. Computation of additional interest:	

Name______________________________
Class Time__________________________

PROBLEM 9-8 or 9-8A

Year	Principal at Beginning of Year	Interest Factor	Accumulated at End of Period
1998			
1999			
2000			
2001			
2002			

Name______________________________

Class Time__________________________

PROBLEM 9-10 or 9-10A

1998			Debit	Credit
1.				
2.				
3.				
4.				

Name___________________________________
Class Time_______________________________

PROBLEM 9-11 or 9-11A

Memorandum to ______________________
Date:
To:
From:
Subject:

Name______________________________
Class Time__________________________

PROBLEM 9-12 or 9-12A

	a. Interest Is Paid When The Loan Is Due	b. Interest Is Deducted In Advance
1. Face value of the note		
2. Effective interest rate		

3a. 1998			Debit	Credit
Jul.	1			
Dec.	31			
1999				
Jul.	1			
b.				
1998				
Jul.	1			
Dec.	31			
1999				
Jul.	1			

PROBLEM 9-12 or 9-12A continued

4. **Balance sheet presentation:**	
a.	
b.	

Name________________________________
Class Time____________________________

PROBLEM 9-13 or 9-13A

1. **Items To Be Recorded**	2. **Items Not To Be Recorded**

Name______________________________________

Class Time_________________________________

PROBLEM 9-15 or 9-15A

Option a:
Option b:
Option c:
Choice:

Name________________________________
Class Time____________________________

EXERCISE 10-1

Issued At	Cash Interest	Interest Expense	Amortization Discount/Premium	Carrying Value
1. Discount				
2. Premium				

EXERCISE 10-2

	Market Rate of Interest		
	(a) 8%	(b) 6%	(c) 10%
1. Amount due at maturity			
2. Cash interest paid			
3. Issue price			

EXERCISE 10-3

a. 500 bonds; $1,000 face value; 8% stated rate; 5 years; annual interest payments:	

b. 500 bonds; $1,000 face value; 8% stated rate; 5 years; semiannual interest payments:	

Name________________________________

Class Time___________________________

EXERCISE 10-3 continued

c. 800 bonds; $1,000 face value; 6% stated rate; 10 years; semiannual interest payments:

d. 2,000 bonds; $50 face value; 12% stated rate; 15 years; semiannual interest payments:

EXERCISE 10-5

1. Calculation of gain or loss on the early redemption of the bonds:

2. Description of gain or loss on the income statement and in the notes:

EXERCISE 10-6

2008			Debit	Credit
Mar.	31			

Name______________________________
Class Time__________________________

EXERCISE 10-7

1. Calculation of present value of minimum lease payments:	

2. Explanation of why $60,000 is not recorded:

EXERCISE 10-8

1. Calculation of annual lease payment:	

2. Amortization table to determine balance sheet presentation:

Date	Lease Payment	Interest Expense	Reduction of Obligation	Lease Obligation
01/01/98				
12/31/98				
12/31/99				

EXERCISE 10-9

1. a.
b.

2a. 1998			Debit	Credit
Jan.	1			

Name________________________________
Class Time__________________________

EXERCISE 10-9 continued

2b. 1998			Debit	Credit
Dec.	31			
2c.				
Dec.	31			

2d. Presentation of lease obligation on the balance sheet:	

EXERCISE 10-11

Balance of deferred tax account:	
1998:	
1999:	
2000:	

Name______________________________
Class Time___________________________

EXERCISE 10-11 continued

Balance of deferred tax account:	
2001:	
2002:	

EXERCISE 10-13

Item	Reported as Operating (O); Investing (I); Financing (F); or Not Separately Reported on SCF (N)
Proceeds from issuance of bonds payable	
Interest expense	
Redemption of bonds payable at maturity	

EXERCISE 10-14

1. How the transaction is reported on the statement of cash flows:

2. Item	Reported as Operating (O); Investing (I); Financing (F); or Not Separately Reported on SCF (N)
Reduction of lease obligation	
Interest expense	
Depreciation expense—leased assets	

Name____________________

Class Time____________________

EXERCISE 10-15

Item	Reported as Operating (O); Investing (I); Financing (F); or Not Separately Reported on SCF (N)	If Operating, Added or Deducted From Net Income
Decrease in taxes payable		
Increase in deferred taxes		

EXERCISE 10-16

1. Calculation of issue price of bonds:	

1998			Debit	Credit
Jan.	1			

2. Effect on issue price if market rate is higher:

3.1998			Debit	Credit
Jul.	1			

4.1998			Debit	Credit
Dec.	31			

Name_______________________________
Class Time___________________________

EXERCISE 10-17

1. 1998			Debit	Credit
Jan.	1			

Balance sheet presentation:	

2. 1998			Debit	Credit
Dec.	31			

Balance sheet presentation:	

3. Explanation of issue price of bonds:

EXERCISE 10-18

1. 1998			Debit	Credit
Jan.	1			

Name____________________________________
Class Time________________________________

EXERCISE 10-18 continued

1. continued. Balance sheet presentation:	

2. 1998			Debit	Credit
Dec.	31			

Balance sheet presentation:	

3. Explanation of issue price of bonds:

Name______________________________
Class Time__________________________

PROBLEM 10-1 or 10-1A

1. a. Bond issue price and explanation:

   b. Bond issue price and explanation:

2. a. Calculation of issue price of bonds:

   b. Calculation of issue price of bonds:

Name__________________________
Class Time__________________________

PROBLEM 10-2 or 10-2A

1.	Discount Amortization – Effective Interest Method of Amortization			
Date	**Cash Interest**	**Interest Expense**	**Discount Amortized**	**Carrying Value**
01/01/98				
12/31/98				
12/31/99				
12/31/00				
12/31/01				
12/31/02				
Totals				

2. **Totals Over The Life Of The Bonds**	
Interest expense	
Cash interest payment	
Discount amortized	

3.2000			Debit	Credit
Dec.	31			

Balance sheet presentation:	

Name______________________________
Class Time______________________________

PROBLEM 10-3 or 10-3A

1.	**Premium Amortization** - Effective Interest Method of Amortization			
Date	**Cash Interest**	**Interest Expense**	**Premium Amortized**	**Carrying Value**
01/01/98				
12/31/98				
12/31/99				
12/31/00				
12/31/01				
12/31/02				
Totals				

2. **Totals Over The Life Of The Bonds**	
Interest expense	
Cash interest payment	
Premium amortized	

3.2000			Debit	Credit
Dec.	31			

Balance sheet presentation:	

Name_______________________________
Class Time__________________________

PROBLEM 10-4 or 10-4A

1. Calculation of gain or loss on early redemption:

2. Calculation of gain or loss on redemption:

3. Presentation of gain or loss on financial statements:

4. Explanation of call price higher than 100:

Name______________________________

Class Time__________________________

PROBLEM 10-5 or 10-5A

1.	Lease Amortization – Effective Interest Method of Amortization			
Date	**Lease Payment**	**Interest Expense**	**Reduction of Obligation**	**Lease Obligation**
01/01/98				
12/31/98				
12/31/99				
12/31/00				
12/31/01				
12/31/02				

2.1998			Debit	Credit
Jan.	1			

3.1999			Debit	Credit
Dec.	31			
Dec.	31			

4. Balance sheet presentation:

Name______________________________

Class Time__________________________

PROBLEM 10-6 or 10-6A

1.1998			Debit	Credit
Dec.	31			

2. Explanations:

Name____________________

Class Time____________________

PROBLEM 10-7

1. Calculation of yearly tax payments:

Year 1:

Year 2:

Year 3:

2. Calculation of income tax expense:

Year 1:

Year 2:

Year 3:

3. Deferred tax account calculation:

Year	Income Tax Expense	Income Tax Payable	Difference	Deferred Tax Account Balance
1996				
1997				
1998				

Name______________________________

Class Time__________________________

PROBLEM 10-7A

1. Calculation of yearly tax payments:

Year 1:

Year 2:

Year 3:

2. Deferred tax account calculation:

Year	Income Tax Expense	Income Tax Payable	Difference	Deferred Tax Account Balance
1				
2				
3				

Name________________________________
Class Time____________________________

PROBLEM 10-8 or 10-8A

1. 1996			Debit	Credit
Dec.	31			
1997				
Dec.	31			
1998				
Dec.	31			

2.

Prepaid/Accrued Pension Cost

The balance represents a(n)________________________________.

3. Effects of pension expense:
Effects of funding payment:
Effects of balance in Prepaid/Accrued Pension Cost account:

Name____________________________
Class Time________________________

PROBLEM 10-9

1. 1998			Debit	Credit
Apr.	1			

2. 1998			Debit	Credit
Oct.	1			

3. Explanation of need for additional interest:

Impact on amounts paid on April 1:

4. Cash flows as a result of the bonds:

Name______________________________
Class Time__________________________

PROBLEM 10-9A

1. 1998			Debit	Credit
Jul.	1			

Calculation of bond issue price:	

2. 1998			Debit	Credit
Dec.	31			

3. 1999			Debit	Credit
Jan.	1			

4. 2004			Debit	Credit
Jul.	1			

Name______________________________
Class Time__________________________

PROBLEM 10-10 or 10-10A

1. Liabilities section of balance sheet at December 31, 1995:	
Current liabilities:	
Long-term liabilities:	

2. Computation of debt-to-equity ratios:
1994:
1995:
Reaction to change in ratio:

3. Other ratios needed:

Name____________________________
Class Time________________________

EXERCISE 11-16

Transaction	Impact on Statement of Cash Flows Operating (O); Investing (I); Financing (F); Not on SCF (N)
Payment of cash dividend on common stock	
Payment of cash dividend on preferred stock	
Distribution of stock dividend	
Declaration of stock split	

EXERCISE 11-17

1. Calculation of dividends paid during 1998.	

2. Dividend payment on the statement of cash flows:

EXERCISE 11-18

1.			Debit	Credit

Name______________________________
Class Time__________________________

EXERCISE 11-18 continued

2. Owner's equity section of Par's balance sheet at December 31, 1998:		

EXERCISE 11-19

Calculation of Capital Account Balances	**Lewis**	**Jamal**	**Lapin**
Beginning balance			

Name____________________________

Class Time________________________

PROBLEM 11-1 or 11-1A

______________ COMPANY

PARTIAL BALANCE SHEET

AS OF DECEMBER 31, 1998

Calculation of amounts for balance sheet:

Account	Calculations	Amount
Preferred Stock		
Additional Paid-in Capital - Preferred Stock		
Common Stock		
Additional Paid-in Capital - Common Stock		
Treasury Stock		
Additional Paid-in Capital - Treasury Stock		
Preferred dividend		
Common stock dividend		

Name________________________________
Class Time______________________________

PROBLEM 11-2 or 11-2A

1. Comments:

2. Recommendations and justification:

Name________________________________
Class Time___________________________

PROBLEM 11-3 or 11-3A

Type	Preferred Stock	Common Stock
1. Noncumulative, nonparticipating		
2. Cumulative, nonparticipating		
2. Cumulative, participating		

Name________________________________

Class Time____________________________

PROBLEM 11-4 or 11-4A

1. Memorandum to the Board of Directors:

Date:

To: Board of Directors

From:

Subject:

2. Memorandum to the Common Stockholders:

Date:

To: Common Stockholders

From:

Subject:

Name________________________________
Class Time____________________________

PROBLEM 11-5 or 11-5A

1. Effect on stockholders' equity accounts and total stockholders' equity:

Mar. 1:

Apr. 1:

Jun. 1:

Jul. 1:

Sep. 1:

Oct. 1:

Dec. 1:

PROBLEM 11-5 or 11-5A continued

2.

________________ COMPANY
PARTIAL BALANCE SHEET
AS OF DECEMBER 31, 1998

3. Difference between stock dividend and stock split:

Name________________________________

Class Time____________________________

PROBLEM 11-6 or 11-6A

Cash flows from financing activities:	

Explanations for exclusions:

Name________________________________

Class Time____________________________

PROBLEM 11-7 or 11-7A

Net Income	Distribution to Partners	
	Ms.______________	Ms. ______________
1.		
2.		
3.		

Name________________________________
Class Time____________________________

PROBLEM 11-8 or 11-8A

1.			Debit	Credit
May	1			
XXX				
Dec.	31			
Dec.	31			
Dec.	31			

2. Capital account balance at year-end:	

3. Explanation of why the capital account balance is not equal to cash on hand:

Name______________________________

Class Time__________________________

PROBLEM 11-9 or 11-9A

Allocation of net income calculations:	

Allocation to partners:	Partners' Allocations	

Name________________________________
Class Time____________________________

PROBLEM 11-10 or 11-10A

Items	Calculations	Amount
1. Preferred stock issued		
2. Preferred stock outstanding		
3. Average per-share sales price of preferred stock when issued		
4. Par value of the common stock		
5. Average per-share sales price of the common stock when issued		
6. Cost of the treasury stock per share		
7. Total stockholders' equity		
8. Per-share book value of the common stock		

Name______________________________
Class Time__________________________

PROBLEM 11-11

1. Effect on balance sheet:			
	Assets =	Liabilities +	Owners' Equity
a.			
b.			
c.			
d.			
e.			
f.			

2. Owners' equity section of the balance sheet:

3. Explanation of the number of shares of stock issued and outstanding at year-end:

Name______________________________
Class Time______________________________

PROBLEM 11-11A

1. Effect on balance sheet:

	Assets =	Liabilities +	Owners' Equity
a.			
b.			
c.			
d.			
e.			

2. Difference between contributed capital and retained earnings:

3. Calculation of book value of common stock:

Name________________________________
Class Time____________________________

PROBLEM 11-12

IVES, INC.
BALANCE SHEET
AS OF XXX

Assets:		
Liabilities:		
Owners' Equity:		

2. Explanation of negative retained earnings balance:

Name______________________________

Class Time__________________________

PROBLEM 11-12A

1.

GRAINFIELD, INC.
PARTIAL BALANCE SHEET
AS OF XXX

2. Explanation of why some of the listed accounts are not shown in the owners' equity section:

Harcourt Brace & Company

Name______________________________

Class Time__________________________

PROBLEM 11-13

1. Cash flows from financing activities:

Explanation for exclusion of any transactions:

2. **Book value per share of common stock:**

May 31, 1995	**May 31,1994**

3. Reaction to the change in book value:

Limitations of book value:

Name______________________________
Class Time__________________________

PROBLEM 11-13A

1. Cash flows from financing activities:

Explanation for exclusion of any transactions:

2. **Book value per share of common stock:**

December 31, 1995	**December 31, 1994**

3. Reaction to change in book value:

Limitations on the use of book value:

Name________________________________
Class Time____________________________

EXERCISE 12-1

1.

FCL COMPANY
INCOME STATEMENT
FOR THE YEAR ENDED DECEMBER 31, 1998

2. Calculation of gross profit percentage:

Explanation of ratio:

EXERCISE 12-2

1. Location of Income from operating the division and gain on sale:

2. **Discontinued operations:**

Name________________________________

Class Time____________________________

EXERCISE 12-3

1.

EASLEY COMPANY

INCOME STATEMENT

FOR THE YEAR ENDED DECEMBER 31, 1998

2. Difference in income statement if not extraordinary:

EXERCISE 12-4

1.

EASLEY COMPANY

INCOME STATEMENT

FOR THE YEAR ENDED DECEMBER 31, 1998

Name____________________________
Class Time________________________

EXERCISE 12-4 continued

2. Comparison of tax effects:

EXERCISE 12-5

Treated as extraordinary? If not, where it should be reported.
a.
b.
c.
d.
e.
f.
g.
h.
i.
j.

EXERCISE 12-6

1. Depreciation expense under each method:		
Year	**Accelerated**	**Straight-line**

Calculation of cumulative effect:	

2. Calculation of depreciation expense on the 1998 income statement:

Name________________________________

Class Time____________________________

EXERCISE 12-7

Calculation of weighted average number of shares:

Calculation of earnings per share:

EXERCISE 12-8

1. 1998			Debit	Credit
Dec.	31			
Dec.	31			
Dec.	31			

2. Description of presentation on financial statements:

Name_______________________________
Class Time__________________________

EXERCISE 12-9

1. Transactions	Unappropriated Retained Earnings Balance	Total Retained Earnings

2. Available for dividend purposes:

EXERCISE 12-10

RYDE, INC.
STATEMENT OF STOCKHOLDERS' EQUITY
FOR THE YEAR ENDED APRIL 30, 1998

	Common Stock	Additional Paid-in Capital	Retained Earnings	Stockholders' Equity
Balance, May 1, 1997				

EXERCISE 12-11

Response to stockholders' inquiry:

Name______________________________
Class Time__________________________

EXERCISE 12-11 continued

Response to stockholders' inquiry (continued):

Thoughts on the concept of comprehensive income's usefulness in explaining the impact of all events for Ellis:

EXERCISE 12-12

Item	Reported as Operating (O); Investing (I); Financing (F); or Not Separately Reported on SCF (N)	Added or Subtracted
Cumulative effect of a change in principle (decrease in net income)		
Cumulative effect of a change in principle (increase in net income)		
Extraordinary loss		
Extraordinary gain		
Foreign currency translation adjustment		

Brief explanation of classifications:

Name________________________________

Class Time____________________________

EXERCISE 12-13

Cash flow from operating activities:	

EXERCISE 12-14

KING COMPANY INCOME STATEMENT FOR THE YEAR ENDED DECEMBER 31, 1998	
Income from continuing operations	

EXERCISE 12-15

1. ELLIS COMPANY INCOME STATEMENT FOR THE YEAR ENDED DECEMBER 31, 1998	

Name______________________________
Class Time___________________________

EXERCISE 12-15 continued

2. Calculation of gross profit percentage:

Is this ratio favorable?

Other information needed to make decision:

3. Calculation of earnings per share:

Dividends per share:

Percent paid out as dividends:

EXERCISE 12-16

Item	Classification
a.	
b.	
c.	
d.	
e.	
f.	
g.	
h.	
i.	
j.	

Name______________________________

Class Time__________________________

PROBLEM 12-1 or 12-1A

1. Explanation of items to be reported after income from continuing operations:

2. ______________________COMPANY	
INCOME STATEMENT	
FOR THE YEAR ENDED DECEMBER 31, 1998	
Income from continuing operations	

Name ______________________________
Class Time __________________________

PROBLEM 12-2 or 12-2A

1. Treatment of change in depreciation method:

1998 financial statement to report the change:

2. Effect on statement of retained earnings as a result of omission:

Calculation of effect of omission:

Name________________________________
Class Time____________________________

PROBLEM 12-3 or 12-3A

1. Calculation of weighted average number of shares:	
Calculations	**Weighted-average Shares**

Calculation of preferred stock dividend:

Calculation of earnings per share:

2. Explanation:

Name______________________________

Class Time__________________________

PROBLEM 12-4 or 12-4A

1. Response:

2. Answers to questions:

Name________________________________
Class Time____________________________

PROBLEM 12-5 or 12-5A

____________________ COMPANY

STATEMENT OF STOCKHOLDERS' EQUITY

FOR THE YEAR ENDED DECEMBER 31, 1998

	Preferred Stock	Common Stock	Paid-in Capital	Treasury Stock	Retained Earnings
Balance, January 1					

Name________________________________

Class Time__________________________

PROBLEM 12-6 or 12-6A

1. Calculation of comprehensive income:

2. Usefulness of comprehensive income to stockholders:

Name______________________________

Class Time__________________________

PROBLEM 12-7 or 12-7A

1. ______________________________

INCOME STATEMENT

FOR THE YEAR ENDED DECEMBER 31, 1998

Earnings per share:

2. Comparison of dividends and earnings per share:

Name________________________________
Class Time____________________________

PROBLEM 12-8 or 12-8A

Note: Problem 12-8 has no part 2.

1. ____________________ COMPANY	
INCOME STATEMENT	
FOR THE YEAR ENDED DECEMBER 31, 1998	
Earnings per share:	

Calculation of cumulative effect:				
	Year	Old Method	New Method	Difference
	1996			
	1997			

2. Effect of transactions on the statement of cash flows:
Presentation of items on statement of cash flows:

Name______________________________
Class Time__________________________

PROBLEM 12-9

1. 1998			Debit	Credit
Dec.	31			

2\. **WEAVER COMPANY**
INCOME STATEMENT
FOR THE YEAR ENDED DECEMBER 31, 1998

3\. **WEAVER COMPANY**
STATEMENT OF RETAINED EARNINGS
FOR THE YEAR ENDED DECEMBER 31, 1998

Beginning balance, January 1, 1998	

4\. Goodwill amortization on the statement of cash flows:

Name________________________________

Class Time____________________________

PROBLEM 12-9A

1. 1998			Debit	Credit
Dec.	31			

2.

LOOMAN COMPANY
STATEMENT OF RETAINED EARNINGS
FOR THE YEAR ENDED DECEMBER 31, 1998

Beginning balance, January 1, 1998	

3. Depreciation error on the statement of cash flows:

Name__________________________________
Class Time________________________________

PROBLEM 12-10 or 12-10A

Note: Problem 12-10 has no part 4.

1. ____________________________ COMPANY

INCOME STATEMENT

FOR THE YEAR ENDED DECEMBER 31, 1998

Earnings per share:

Calculation of cumulative effect:

PROBLEM 12-10 or 12-10A continued

2. Which income number to predict income?

3. ______________________ COMPANY

STATEMENT OF RETAINED EARNINGS

FOR THE YEAR ENDED DECEMBER 31, 1998

Retained earnings, January 1, 1998

4. Effect of items on balance sheet accounts:

Item a:

Item b:

Item c:

Name____________________________
Class Time_________________________

EXERCISE 13-1

1. 1998			Debit	Credit
Jan.	1			
Jun.	30			
Dec.	31			
1999				
Jan.	1			

2. Explanation of ability to sell bonds at 102:

EXERCISE 13-2

1. 1998			Debit	Credit
Jan.	1			

Note: Complete the table below to help you prepare the entry for part 2.

2. **Straight-line Method of Amortization**

Date	Cash Interest	Interest Income	Premium/Discount Amortized	Carrying Value
01/01/98				
12/31/98				

Name________________________________

Class Time____________________________

EXERCISE 13-2 continued

2. 1998			Debit	Credit
Dec.	31			

3. Explanation of purchase of bonds at less than when they mature:

EXERCISE 13-3

1. 1998			Debit	Credit
Jan.	1			

Note: Complete the table below to help you prepare the entry for part 2.

2.	Effective Interest Method of Amortization			
Date	**Cash Interest**	**Interest Income**	**Premium/Discount Amortized**	**Carrying Value**
01/01/98				
12/31/98				

2. 1998			Debit	Credit
Dec.	31			

3. Explanation of purchase of bonds at less than when they mature:

Name________________________________

Class Time____________________________

EXERCISE 13-4

1. 1998			Debit	Credit
Jan.	2			

Note: Complete the table below to help you prepare the entry for part 2.

2.	Straight-line Method of Amortization			
Date	**Cash Interest**	**Interest Income**	**Premium/Discount Amortized**	**Carrying Value**
01/02/98				
12/31/98				

2. 1998			Debit	Credit
Dec.	31			

3. Explanation of willingness to pay more for bonds than when they mature:

EXERCISE 13-5

1. 1998			Debit	Credit
Jan.	2			

Note: Complete the table below to help you prepare the entry for part 2.

2.	Effective Interest Method of Amortization			
Date	**Cash Interest**	**Interest Income**	**Premium/Discount Amortized**	**Carrying Value**
01/02/98				
12/31/98				

Name________________________________

Class Time____________________________

EXERCISE 13-5 continued

2. continued; 1998			Debit	Credit
Dec.	31			

3. Explanation of willingness to pay more for bonds than when they mature:

EXERCISE 13-6

Complete this amortization table to help you calculate the carrying value of the bonds.

1. and 2.	Straight-line Method of Amortization			
Date	**Cash Interest**	**Interest Income**	**Premium/Discount Amortized**	**Carrying Value**
1/02/98				
6/30/98				
12/31/98				
6/30/99				
12/31/99				

1. Carrying value of bonds on 7/1/98 from table: ____________________
2. Carrying value of bonds on 12/31/99 from table: ____________________

EXERCISE 13-7

Complete this amortization table to help you calculate the carrying value of the bonds.

1. and 2.	Effective Interest Method of Amortization			
Date	**Cash Interest**	**Interest Income**	**Premium/Discount Amortized**	**Carrying Value**
1/02/98				
6/30/98				
12/31/98				
6/30/99				
12/31/99				

1. Carrying value of bonds on 6/30/98 from table: ____________________
2. Carrying value of bonds on 12/31/99 from table: ____________________

Name________________________________

Class Time____________________________

EXERCISE 13-8

1. Classification of stock and explanation of why:

2. 1998			Debit	Credit
Dec.	1			
Dec.	20			
Dec.	31			
1999				
Jan.	15			
Feb.	12			

3. Classification at December 31, 1998:

EXERCISE 13-9

1. Classification of stock and explanation of why:

Name______________________
Class Time__________________

EXERCISE 13-9 continued

2. 1998			Debit	Credit
Aug.	15			
Dec.	31			
1999				
Jul.	8			

3. Classification at December 31, 1998:

EXERCISE 13-10

1. Explanation of amount to report investment at December 31, 1998:

Investment in Roberts

Name________________________________
Class Time____________________________

EXERCISE 13-10 continued

2. Calculation of gain or loss on sale of stock on January 10, 1999:

EXERCISE 13-11

1. Calculation of cash to report on a post-merger balance sheet on June 13, 1998:

2. Calculation of goodwill resulting from the purchase:

EXERCISE 13-12

1. Type of business combination and explanation:

2. Amount at which Keller should record the real estate:

Name______________________________
Class Time__________________________

EXERCISE 13-12 continued

3. Computation of goodwiil resulting from the purchase:	

4. Why would Keller pay more than fair value?

EXERCISE 13-13

Situation	Amount of Foreign Exchange Gain or Loss	Gain or Loss?
1.		
2.		
3.		
4.		

Name________________________
Class Time______________________

EXERCISE 13-14

1. Calculation of total assets:

2. Calculation of translation adjustment:

3. Interpretation of translation adjustment:

Effect of translation adjustment on subsidiary's net income and cash flow:

EXERCISE 13-15

Investment	Accounted For and Reported: Trading Security (T); Available-for-Sale (AS); Equity Investee (E); or Subsidiary in Consolidated Statements (S)
1.	
2.	
3.	
4.	
5.	

EXERCISE 13-16

Investment	Accounted For and Reported: Held-to-Maturity Security (HM); Trading Security (T); Available-for-Sale Security (AS)
1.	
2.	
3.	
4.	
5.	

Name

Class Time

PROBLEM 13-1 or 13-1A

1. Type of business combination and explanation:

2. Calculation of goodwill:

3. 1998

			Debit	Credit
Mar.	1			

4. Effect on goodwill:

Importance of reliable estimates:

Name

Class Time

PROBLEM 13-2 or 13-2A

1. Type of business combination and explanation:

2. 1998			Debit	Credit

3. Calculation of goodwill:

4. Calculation of consolidated cash balance:

Calculation of consolidated land balance:

PROBLEM 13-2 or 13-2A continued

4.

____

CONSOLIDATED BALANCE SHEET

______________, 1998

(ALL AMOUNTS IN MILLIONS OF DOLLARS)

Assets

Liabilities

Stockholders' Equity

Name ______________________________

Class Time __________________________

PROBLEM 13-3 or 13-3A

1. Type of business combination and explanation:

2. 1998			Debit	Credit
Jan.	1			

Calculation of purchase price:

3. ______________, INC. AND ______________, INC.

BALANCE SHEETS

JANUARY 1, 1998

(ALL AMOUNTS IN MILLIONS OF DOLLARS)

	__________, Inc.	________, Inc.
Current assets		
Current liabilities		

PROBLEM 13-3 or 13-3A continued

4. ________________ AND SUBSIDIARY

CONSOLIDATED BALANCE SHEET

JANUARY 1, 1998

(ALL AMOUNTS IN MILLIONS OF DOLLARS)

Assets

Liabilities

Stockholders' Equity

5. Accounting treatment of goodwill:

Name____________________________

Class Time____________________________

PROBLEM 13-4 or 13-4A

1. 1998			Debit	Credit
Jan.	5			
Jan.	12			
Jan.	15			
Jan.	18			
Jan.	25			
Jan.	30			
Jan.	31			

2. Calculation of foreign exchange gain or loss:	

PROBLEM 13-4 or 13-4A continued

3. Explanation of how a company can do business with foreign suppliers and customers but avoid foreign currency risks:

Name___________________________
Class Time______________________

PROBLEM 13-5 or 13-5A

1. ______________________________

INCOME STATEMENT

FOR THE YEAR ENDED DECEMBER 31, 1998

	Foreign Currency ________	Exchange Rate	U. S. Dollars

2. ______________________________

BALANCE SHEET

AS OF DECEMBER 31, 1998

Assets	Foreign Currency ________	Exchange Rate	U. S. Dollars
Current assets:			
Liabilities and Stockholders' Equity			

PROBLEM 13-5 or 13-5A continued

3. Comments on necessity of Translation Adjustment account:

Is it an addition to or deduction from stockholders' equity:

Cash flow implications to the parent from the adjustment:

Name________________________________

Class Time___________________________

PROBLEM 13-6 or 13-6A

1. 1998			Debit	Credit
Jul.	1			
Oct.	23			
Nov.	21			
Dec.	10			
Dec.	28			
Dec.	31			
Dec.	31			

Calculation of unrealized gain or loss at 12/31/98:

Security	Total Cost	Total Fair Value	Gain (Loss)

PROBLEM 13-6 or 13-6A continued

2. Partial balance sheet at December 31, 1998:

3. Items on the income statement:

Name______________________________
Class Time__________________________

PROBLEM 13-7 or 13-7A

1. 1998			Debit	Credit
Jan.	15			
May	23			
Jun.	1			
Oct.	20			
Dec.	15			
Dec.	31			

2. Total income from investments during 1998:

3. Change in answer to part 2 if categorized as trading securities and explanation:

Name____________________________
Class Time________________________

PROBLEM 13-8 or 13-8A

1.

____

INCOME STATEMENT

FOR THE YEAR ENDED DECEMBER 31, 1998

	Millions of ________	Exchange Rate	U. S. Dollars

Explanation of the necessity to translate the statement:

2. Calculation of investor's share of investee's income:

3.

Investment in ________________

Name________________________________
Class Time____________________________

PROBLEM 13-9 or 13-9A

PARTIAL BALANCE SHEET
DECEMBER 31, 1998

Assets		

Name________________________________
Class Time____________________________

EXERCISE 14-1

Cash equivalents on the balance sheet at December 31, 1998:	

EXERCISE 14-2

Item	Reported as Operating (O); Investing (I); Financing (F); or Supplemental Schedule (S)	Item	Reported as Operating (O); Investing (I); Financing (F); or Supplemental Schedule (S)
1.		8.	
2.		9.	
3.		10.	
4.		11.	
5.		12.	
6.		13.	
7.			

EXERCISE 14-3

1. 1998			Debit	Credit
Dec.	31			

2. Description of how the bond retirement is reported:

Name______________________________
Class Time___________________________

EXERCISE 14-4

Calculation of cash collections for the year ending December 31, 1998:	

EXERCISE 14-5

Calculation of cash payments for inventory for the year ending December 31, 1998:	

EXERCISE 14-6

1. LABRADOR COMPANY PARTIAL STATEMENT OF CASH FLOWS FOR THE YEAR ENDED DECEMBER 31, 1998	
Cash Flows From Operating Activities	
Net Cash Provided By Operating Activities	

Name____________________________

Class Time________________________

EXERCISE 14-6 continued

Calculation of cash collections from customers:

Calculation of payments to suppliers:

Calculation of cash paid for general and administrative expenses:

Cash paid for interest:

Cash paid for taxes:

2. What does the direct method reveal that the indirect method does not?

Name________________________________
Class Time___________________________

EXERCISE 14-7

Case 1:

Accounts Receivable

Case 2:

Inventory

Accounts Payable

Case 3:

Prepaid Insurance

Case 4:

Income Taxes Payable

Name____________________
Class Time____________________

EXERCISE 14-8

1.

Retained Earnings

Dividends Payable

2. Should the stock dividend appear on the statement of cash flows?

EXERCISE 14-9

Item	Added to Net Income (A); Deducted From Net Income (D); Not Reported in the Operating Section (N)	Item	Added to Net Income (A); Deducted From Net Income (D); Not Reported in the Operating Section (N)
1.		6.	
2.		7.	
3.		8.	
4.		9.	
5.		10.	

Name________________________________

Class Time__________________________

EXERCISE 14-10

1. SALVATORE COMPANY PARTIAL STATEMENT OF CASH FLOWS FOR THE YEAR ENDED DECEMBER 31, 1998	
Cash Flows From Operating Activities	
Net Cash Provided By Operating Activities	

2. Explanation of why cash flows from operating activities is more or less than net income:

EXERCISE 14-11

Transaction	How Reported on the Statement of Cash Flows	Transaction	How Reported on the Statement of Cash Flows
1.		6.	
2.		7.	
3.		8.	
4.		9.	
5.		10.	

Name______________________________
Class Time______________________________

EXERCISE 14-12

Transaction	How Reported on the Statement of Cash Flows	Transaction	How Reported on the Statement of Cash Flows
1.		7.	
2.		8.	
3.		9.	
4.		10.	
5.		11.	
6.		12.	

EXERCISE 14-13

Calculation of accumulated depreciation on the assets sold:

Accumulated Depreciation

Calculation of acquisitions of plant assets:

Plant and Equipment

Calculation of acquisitions of patents:

Patents

Name________________________________
Class Time______________________________

EXERCISE 14-13 continued

Cash Flows From Operating Activities	
Cash Flows From Investing Activities	

EXERCISE 14-14

1. **HANDSOME HOUNDS GROOMING COMPANY**
INCOME STATEMENT
FOR THE YEAR ENDED XX/XX/XX

Name________________________________

Class Time____________________________

EXERCISE 14-14 continued

2. HANDSOME HOUNDS GROOMING COMPANY		
STATEMENT OF CASH FLOWS		
FOR THE YEAR ENDED XX/XX/XX		
Cash Flows from Operating Activities		

3. Explanation of difference between cash flows from operations compared to net income:

Name________________________________
Class Time__________________________

EXERCISE 14-14 continued

4.

HANDSOME HOUNDS GROOMING COMPANY
BALANCE SHEET
AS OF XX/XX/XX

Assets		

Name______________________________

Class Time___________________________

PROBLEM 14-1 or 14-1A

1. Calculations of changes in account balances and explanations:

Account Name	Net Change	Explanation

1. ____________________________COMPANY

STATEMENT OF CASH FLOWS

FOR THE YEAR ENDED DECEMBER 31, 1998

Cash Flows from Operating Activities		

PROBLEM 14-1 or 14-1A continued

2. Comments on cash:

Name____________________

Class Time____________________

PROBLEM 14-2 or 14-2A

1. **Statement of Cash Flows Work Sheet**

Accounts	Balances 12/31/98	Balances 12/31/97	Changes	Cash Inflows (Outflows) Operating	Cash Inflows (Outflows) Investing	Cash Inflows (Outflows) Financing
Cash						
Accounts receivable						
Inventory						
Prepaid rent						
Land						
Plant and equipment						
Accumulated depreciation						
Accounts payable						
Income taxes payable						
Short-term notes payable						
Bonds payable						
Common stock						
Retained earnings						
Totals						

2. ____________________COMPANY

STATEMENT OF CASH FLOWS

FOR THE YEAR ENDED DECEMBER 31, 1998

Cash Flows from Operating Activities

PROBLEM 14-2 or 14-2A continued

3. Comments on cash:

Name_______________________________

Class Time__________________________

PROBLEM 14-3 or 14-3A

1. Calculations of income statement items to cash basis:

Income Statement Items	Amount	Adjustment	Cash Flows

1. Calculations of changes in account balances and explanations:

Account Name	Net Change	Explanation

1. ____________________________CORP.

STATEMENT OF CASH FLOWS

FOR THE YEAR ENDED DECEMBER 31, 1998

Cash Flows from Operating Activities		

Name ______________________________
Class Time __________________________

PROBLEM 14-3 or 14-3A continued

2. Memorandum to the president:		
TO:	President of __________________ Corp.	
FROM:		
DATE:		
SUBJECT:	Cash flows	

Name________________________________

Class Time____________________________

PROBLEM 14-4 or 14-4A

1. Calculations of changes in account balances and explanations:

Account Name	Net Change	Explanation

PROBLEM 14-4 or 14-4A continued

1. ______________________________ CORP.

STATEMENT OF CASH FLOWS

FOR THE YEAR ENDED DECEMBER 31, 1998

Cash Flows from Operating Activities		

Name________________________________

Class Time____________________________

PROBLEM 14-4 or 14-4A continued

2. Memorandum to the president:

TO: President of ____________________ Corp.

FROM:

DATE:

SUBJECT: Cash flows

Name________________________________
Class Time____________________________

PROBLEM 14-5 or 14-5A

1.	Statement of Cash Flows Work Sheet					
	---------Balances--------			--------Cash Inflows (Outflows)------		
Accounts	**12/31/98**	**12/31/97**	**Changes**	**Operating**	**Investing**	**Financing**
Cash						
Accounts receivable						
Inventory						
Prepayments						
Land						
Plant and equipment						
Accumulated depreciation						
Accounts payable						
Other accrued liabilities						
Income taxes payable						
Long-term bank loan payable						
Common stock						
Retained earnings						
Totals						

2. ____________________________CORP.		
STATEMENT OF CASH FLOWS		
FOR THE YEAR ENDED DECEMBER 31, 1998		
Cash Flows from Operating Activities		

PROBLEM 14-5 or 14-5A continued

3. Memorandum to the president:

TO: President of ____________________ Corp.

FROM:

DATE:

SUBJECT: Cash flows

Name______________________________
Class Time____________________________

PROBLEM 14-6 or 14-6A

1. Calculations of changes in account balances and explanations:

Account Name	Net Change	Explanation

Calculations of income statement items to cash basis:

Income Statement Items	Amount	Adjustment	Cash Flows

1. ______________________________INC.

STATEMENT OF CASH FLOWS

FOR THE YEAR ENDED DECEMBER 31, 1998

Cash Flows from Operating Activities		

Name________________________________
Class Time____________________________

PROBLEM 14-6 or 14-6A continued

2. Memorandum to the president:

TO: President of ____________________, Inc.

FROM:

DATE:

SUBJECT: Cash flows

Name______________________________
Class Time__________________________

PROBLEM 14-7 or 14-7A

1. Calculations of changes in account balances and explanations:		
Account Name	**Net Change**	**Explanation**

PROBLEM 14-7 or 14-7A continued

1. ______________________________INC.

STATEMENT OF CASH FLOWS

FOR THE YEAR ENDED DECEMBER 31, 1998

Cash Flows from Operating Activities

Name______________________________

Class Time__________________________

PROBLEM 14-7 or 14-7A continued

2. Memorandum to the president:	
TO:	President of _________________ , Inc.
FROM:	
DATE:	
SUBJECT:	Cash flows

Name____________________________
Class Time_______________________

PROBLEM 14-8 or 14-8A

1.	Statement of Cash Flows Work Sheet					
	---------Balances--------			--------Cash Inflows (Outflows)------		
Accounts	**12/31/98**	**12/31/97**	**Changes**	**Operating**	**Investing**	**Financing**
Cash						
Accounts receivable						
Inventory						
Prepayments						
Land						
Plant and equipment						
Accumulated depreciation						
Accounts payable						
Other accrued liabilities						
Interest payable						
Long-term bank loan payable						
Common stock						
Retained earnings						
Totals						

PROBLEM 14-8 or 14-8A continued

2. ______________________INC.

STATEMENT OF CASH FLOWS

FOR THE YEAR ENDED DECEMBER 31, 1998

Cash Flows from Operating Activities

Name______________________________

Class Time______________________________

PROBLEM 14-8 or 14-8A continued

3. Memorandum to the president:	
TO:	President of __________________ , Inc.
FROM:	
DATE:	
SUBJECT:	Cash flows

Name____________________________
Class Time________________________

PROBLEM 14-9 or 14-9A

1. Calculations of changes in account balances and explanations:

Account Name	Net Change	Explanation

1. __________________________ COMPANY

STATEMENT OF CASH FLOWS

FOR THE YEAR ENDED DECEMBER 31, 1998

Cash Flows from Operating Activities		

2. ______________________ COMPANY

BALANCE SHEET

DECEMBER 31, 1998

Assets

3. Responses to cash issues:

Name________________________________

Class Time____________________________

PROBLEM 14-10 or 14-10A

1. ____________________ COMPANY		
BALANCE SHEET		
DECEMBER 31, 1998		
Assets		

2. **Statement of Cash Flows Work Sheet**

	---------Balances--------			--------Cash Inflows (Outflows)------		
Accounts	**12/31/98**	**12/31/97**	**Changes**	**Operating**	**Investing**	**Financing**
Cash						
Accounts receivable						
Land						
Plant and equipment						
Accumulated depreciation						
Investments						
Current liabilities						
Bonds payable						
Common stock						
Retained earnings						
Totals						

PROBLEM 14-10 or 14-10A continued

3. ______________________________ COMPANY

STATEMENT OF CASH FLOWS

FOR THE YEAR ENDED DECEMBER 31, 1998

Cash Flows from Operating Activities

4. Possible explanation of bond transaction:

Name_______________________________
Class Time__________________________

PROBLEM 14-11 or 14-11A

1. Calculations of changes in account balances and explanations:

Account Name	Net Change	Explanation

Calculations of income statement items to cash basis:

Income Statement Items	Amount	Adjustment	Cash Flows

PROBLEM 14-11 or 14-11A continued

1. ______________________________ CORP.

STATEMENT OF CASH FLOWS

FOR THE YEAR ENDED JUNE 30, 1998

Cash Flows from Operating Activities

2. Evaluation of statement about cash flows:

Name________________________________

Class Time____________________________

PROBLEM 14-12 or 14-12A

1. Calculations of changes in account balances and explanations:

Account Name	Net Change	Explanation

PROBLEM 14-12 or 14-12A continued

1. ______________________ CORP.

STATEMENT OF CASH FLOWS

FOR THE YEAR ENDED JUNE 30, 1998

Cash Flows from Operating Activities

2. Evaluation of statement about cash flows:

Name

Class Time

PROBLEM 14-13 or 14-13A

1. Are the U. S. Treasury bills cash equivalents? If not, how are they classified? Explain.

2. Calculations of changes in account balances and explanations:

(Amounts in Thousands of Dollars)

Account Name	Net Change	Explanation

Calculations of income statement items to cash basis:

(Amounts in Thousands of Dollars)

Income Statement Items	Amount	Adjustment	Cash Flows

PROBLEM 14-13 or 14-13A continued

Calculations of income statement items to cash basis (continued)			
(Amounts in Thousands of Dollars)			
Income Statement Items	Amount	Adjustment	Cash Flows

1. ____________________________COMPANY

STATEMENT OF CASH FLOWS

FOR THE YEAR ENDED DECEMBER 31, 1998

(Amounts in Thousands of Dollars)

Cash Flows from Operating Activities		

Name______________________________
Class Time__________________________

EXERCISE 15-1

1. Accounts receivable turnover ratio:		
Year	**Calculations**	**Answer**
1998		
1997		

2. Number of days' sales in receivables:		
Year	**Calculations**	**Answer**
1998		
1997		

3. Comments on the efficiency of Faraway's collection efforts:

EXERCISE 15-2

1. Inventory turnover ratio:		
Year	**Calculations**	**Answer**
1998		
1997		

Name________________________________
Class Time____________________________

EXERCISE 15-2 continued

2. Number of days' sales in inventory:

Year	Calculations	Answer
1998		
1997		

3. Comments on the company's management of inventory over the two years:

What problems do you see?

EXERCISE 15-3

1. a. Accounts receivable turnover ratio:

Company	Calculations	Answer
General Motors		
Ford		
Chrysler		

1. b. Number of days' sales in receivables:

Company	Calculations	Answer
General Motors		
Ford		
Chrysler		

Name______________________________
Class Time__________________________

EXERCISE 15-3 continued

1. c. Inventory turnover ratio:		
Company	**Calculations**	**Answer**
General Motors		
Ford		
Chrysler		

1. d. Number of days' sales in inventory:		
Company	**Calculations**	**Answer**
General Motors		
Ford		
Chrysler		

1. e. Cash to cash operating cycle:		
Company	**Calculations**	**Answer**
General Motors		
Ford		
Chrysler		

2. Comments on the liquidity of these three companies:

Name______________________________
Class Time__________________________

EXERCISE 15-4

1.	Coca-Cola	Pepsi
a. Current ratio		
b. Quick assets Acid-test or Quick ratio		

2. Comments on the liquidity of the two companies:
3. Other ratios that may be helpful to assess liquidity:

EXERCISE 15-5

1.	McDonald's	Wendy's
a. Working capital		
b. Current ratio		
c. Quick assets Acid-test or Quick ratio		

Harcourt Brace & Company

Name________________________________
Class Time____________________________

EXERCISE 15-5 continued

2. Comments on the liquidity of the two companies:

3.	McDonald's	Wendy's
Cash flow from operations to current liabilities ratio:		

How does this information change your opinion as to the relative liquidity of each company?

4. Steps possible to cover short-term cash requirements:

Name________________________________

Class Time___________________________

EXERCISE 15-6

1.	1995	1994
a. Debt-to-equity		
b. Times interest earned		
c. Debt service coverage		
d. Cash flow from operations to capital expenditures		

2. Comments on the company's solvency:

EXERCISE 15-7

1.	12/31/98	12/31/97
a. Debt-to-equity		

b. Times interest earned for 1998:	
c. Debt service coverage for 1998:	

Name____________________________
Class Time____________________________

EXERCISE 15-7 continued

2. Comments on the company's solvency:
Difference in ratios in terms of indication of ability to pay debts:

EXERCISE 15-8

1.	Calculations	Answer
a. Return on sales		
b. Asset turnover		
c. Return on assets		
d. Return on common stockholders' equity		

2. Comments on the company's use of leverage:
Has it successfully used leverage? Explain.

Name________________________________
Class Time______________________________

EXERCISE 15-9

	Calculations	Answer
Case 1: Return on assets		
Case 2: Net sales		
Case 3: Return on assets		
Case 4: Net income		
Case 5: Average total assets		

EXERCISE 15-10

1.	Calculations	Answer
a. Earnings per share		
b. Price/earnings ratio		
c. Dividend payout ratio		
d. Dividend yield ratio		

2. Other information needed before advising a client regarding a purchase:

Name______________________________

Class Time__________________________

EXERCISE 15-11

	Calculations	Answer
1. Earnings per share before extraordinary items		
2. Earnings per share after the extraordinary loss		

3. Comments on which ratio is more useful to management:

Would your answer change if the ratios were to be used by outsiders? Why?

Name______________________________

Class Time__________________________

EXERCISE 15-12

1.

FARINET COMPANY
COMMON-SIZE COMPARATIVE BALANCE SHEETS
DECEMBER 31, 1998 AND 1997

	12/31/98		12/31/97	
	Dollars	Percent	Dollars	Percent

2. Observations about changes in composition:

Name________________________________

Class Time____________________________

EXERCISE 15-12 continued

3.

FARINET COMPANY
COMPARATIVE BALANCE SHEETS
DECEMBER 31, 1998 AND 1997

	December 31		Increase (Decrease)	
	1998	1997	Dollars	Percent

4. Items with Largest Change	Refer To

Name____________________________

Class Time____________________________

EXERCISE 15-13

1.

MARINERS CORP.
COMMON-SIZE COMPARATIVE INCOME STATEMENTS
FOR THE YEARS ENDED DECEMBER 31, 1998 AND 1997

	1998		1997	
	Dollars	**Percent**	**Dollars**	**Percent**

2. Observations:

Name_______________________________
Class Time__________________________

EXERCISE 15-13 continued

3.

MARINERS CORP.
COMPARATIVE STATEMENTS OF INCOME
FOR THE YEARS ENDED DECEMBER 31, 1998 AND 1997

			Increase (Decrease)	
	1998	1997	Dollars	Percent

4. Items with Largest Change	Refer To

Name______________________________
Class Time______________________________

PROBLEM 15-1

1.	Calculations	Answer
Working capital		
Current ratio		
Quick ratio		

2.	Effect of Transaction On					
Transaction	Working Capital		Current Ratio		Quick Ratio	
	New Amount	Effect	New Ratio	Effect	New Ratio	Effect
a.						
b.						
c.						
d.						
e.						
f.						
g.						
h.						
i.						
j.						
k.						
l.						

Name_______________________________
Class Time__________________________

PROBLEM 15-1A

1.	Calculations	Answer
Debt-to-equity ratio		

2.	Effect of Transaction On Debt-to-Equity Ratio	
Transaction	New Ratio	Effect
a.		
b.		
c.		
d.		
e.		
f.		
g.		
h.		
i.		
j.		
k.		
l.		

Name____________________________
Class Time________________________

PROBLEM 15-2

1.	Calculations	Answer
Working capital		
Current ratio		
Quick ratio		

2.	Effect of Transaction On					
Transaction	Working Capital		Current Ratio		Quick Ratio	
	New Amount	Effect	New Ratio	Effect	New Ratio	Effect
a.						
b.						
c.						
d.						
e.						
f.						
g.						
h.						
i.						
j.						
k.						
l.						

Name______________________________
Class Time__________________________

PROBLEM 15-2A

1.	Calculations	Answer
Debt-to-equity ratio		

2.	Effect of Transaction On Debt-to-Equity Ratio	
Transaction	**New Ratio**	**Effect**
a.		
b.		
c.		
d.		
e.		
f.		
g.		
h.		
i.		
j.		
k.		
l.		

Name________________________________
Class Time____________________________

PROBLEM 15-3 or 15-3A

1.	Calculations	Answer
a. Return on sales		
b. Asset turnover		
c. Return on assets		

2.	Calculations	Answer
Asset turnover needed to achieve goal		

3.	Calculations	Answer
Income needed next year to achieve the goal		

4. Reasonableness of goals:

Focus on what to obtain goals:

Name________________________________

Class Time____________________________

PROBLEM 15-4 or 15-4A

Note: Problem 15-4A has no part 4.

1.	2001	2000	1999
1. Sales			
2. Net income			
3. Dividends declared and paid			
4. Owners' equity			
5. Debt			
6. Return on owners' equity			
7. Debt to total assets			

PROBLEM 15-4 or 15-4A continued

2. Can the CEO meet the requirements? Explain.

3. Alternative actions for the CEO to consider:

4. Reasons the CEO may have for wanting to limit debt:

Name______________________________
Class Time___________________________

PROBLEM 15-5 or 15-5A

1.	**Calculations**	**Answer**
a. Times interest earned		
b. Return on total assets		
c. Return on common stockholders' equity		
d. Debt-equity ratio		
e. Current ratio		
f. Quick ratio		
g. Accounts receivable turnover ratio		
h. Number of days' sales in receivables		
i. Inventory turnover ratio		

PROBLEM 15-5 or 15-5A

1. continued	Calculations	Answer
j. Number of days' sales in inventory		
k. Number of days in cash operating cycle		

2. Comments on the overall financial health of the company:

Name____________________________
Class Time________________________

PROBLEM 15-6 or 15-6A

1.	Calculations	Answer
Sales growth		
Return on stockholders' equity		
Long-term debt-to-equity ratio		
Payment of a cash dividend of 50% of net income		

2. Factors contributing to the failure to meet the objectives:

PROBLEM 15-6 or 15-6A continued

3. Actions to be taken by controller:

Name_______________________________
Class Time__________________________

PROBLEM 15-7

1. **Ratio**	**Industry Average**	**Heartland, Inc.**
Current ratio		
Acid-test (quick) ratio		
Accounts receivable turnover		
Inventory turnover		
Debt-to-equity ratio		
Times interest earned		
Return on sales		
Asset turnover		
Return on assets		
Return on common stockholders' equity		

PROBLEM 15-7 continued

2. Evaluation of the company's ratios:

3. Do you think the bank will approve the loan? Explain.

Name____________________________
Class Time________________________

PROBLEM 15-7A

1. **Ratio**	**Industry Average**	**Midwest, Inc.**
Current ratio		
Acid-test (quick) ratio		
Inventory turnover		
Debt-to-equity ratio		
Times interest earned		
Return on sales		
Asset turnover		
Return on common stockholders' equity		

PROBLEM 15-7A continued

2. Evaluation of the company's ratios:

3. Do you think the bank will approve the loan? Explain.